# FENG SHUI on A DIME

## AFFORDABLE FENG SHUI FOR LOVE, WEALTH, HEALTH AND SUCCESS

### STEPHANIE LIANG

**TRANSFORMIND BOOKS**

FENG SHUI ON A DIME

© 2016 Stephanie Liang

Library of Congress Control Number: 2015959906
ISBN: 978-0-9971155-0-5

Publisher:

TRANSFORMIND
B O O K S

transformindbooks.com

Printed in the United States

Cover Design: AJ Wilson
Interior Design and Illustrations: Leslie Klenke
Editor: Amy Lucas

DISCLAIMER: The ideas, concepts and opinions expressed in this book are intended for educational purposes only. This book is sold with the understanding that the author and publisher are not dispensing medical advice of any kind or prescribing the use of any technique as a form of treatment for physical, emotional or medical problems. This book is not intended to replace medical advice from a licensed physician, nor to diagnose or treat any disease, condition, illness or injury. The intent of the author is only to offer information of a general nature to help you in your quest for emotional and spiritual well-being. In the event you use any of the information in this book for yourself, which is your constitutional right, the author and publisher assume no responsibility for your actions.

# TABLE OF CONTENTS

# INTRODUCTION

Feng shui is an ancient art that has, over the span of 5000 years, weaved into more and more intricate theories, solutions and schools of thought. *Feng Shui on a Dime* makes feng shui accessible, both monetarily and practically. Rather than learning about all the different feng shui schools or getting bogged down in theory and history, you can look at the specific issues you wish to cure as the pendulum in your life sways.

There are five life areas that typically seem to be on our minds. The flux and balance of each may vary: at some points we are more interested in our careers, at others our relationships, but our compass and intent tend to point in one of five directions—**health, wealth, career, love** and **family**.

Many feng shui books focus on the different life areas found on the Ba-gua Map, or Feng Shui Octagon: Wealth, Fame, Marriage, Children, Helpful People, Career, Knowledge and Family. *Feng Shui on a Dime* takes a different approach, focusing on common conundrums and offering simple, inexpensive solutions to affect change in the life areas we want to improve. We explore both traditional fix-its and more contemporary solutions.

We would be remiss if we didn't offer a very basic explanation of the core principles behind feng shui before delving into specific issues and their solutions.

# What Is Feng Shui?

Feng shui is the ancient Chinese art of placement. Practitioners believe that the arrangement of your environment—the placement of surrounding objects; the location and shape of your home; the street you live on; the type of materials your furniture is made of; the colors you use to decorate, and many other intricacies—significantly affects your personal and professional lives.

East and West have comingled long enough now that many of us have heard of chi. According to traditional Chinese culture, chi is the life force that permeates, well…everything. This invisible energy runs through our bodies, our minds, our environments; it is the vibrational play of energy that swirls through our interactions with other people and our surroundings.

Our physical environment can stifle or stimulate our chi, thereby affecting every component of our lives. Feng shui helps to correct blocked chi, opening up a free flow of energy between our self and our universe. Think of feng shui as earth acupuncture. Stimulate the right point, and voila! You've just aligned the earth—with your chi— with your desire.

But is there any scientific basis for a belief in chi?

If we look through the lens of Western science, then no. Empirical effects and subjective experience aren't enough to substantiate that which can't be seen. But if we consider chi in light of physics and not chemistry, we can discover that there is indeed a unity behind all existence and a never-ending exchange between external stimuli and internal reactions.

Newton's Third Law of Classical Mechanics states that "for every action there is an equal and opposite reaction." And quantum mechanics has shown that objects can exert influence without making any direct contact.

Consider the continual interplay of energy between your body and the earth. The earth is electrically charged, and science has shown that when you connect with the earth—standing barefoot on grass let's say—electrons pass from the ground, through the soles of your feet, and into your body. This technique, called grounding or earthing, has been shown to alleviate pain, improve sleep, calm inflammation and elevate well-being.

Science has also shown that humans (and all of existence for that matter) actually radiate visible light. This light is 1000 times less intense than the light levels visible to the naked eye, but some people swear they can see it. Auras sound familiar? Those in the science world refer to it as the biophoton field, and it's been proven to process, store and retrieve information that controls your biological processes.

Healing therapies that access the bioenergetic field—modalities like reiki, acupuncture, acupressure and pranic healing—all attempt to activate and re-balance stifled chi.

## How Does Feng Shui Work Its Magic?

Rearranging the placement of furniture, adding a vibrant green plant to a specific section of your home, painting your front door red—cures such as these can positively impact your life, but not without the most imperative element: *Intention*.

Is placing a red sheet between the mattress and box spring of your bed *really* going to increase your love life? Or is it the positive and determined thought behind such an action that activates change throughout your life? Every feng shui cure should be accompanied by a specific desire and well-planned Intention. Intention is arguably 70% of feng shui's effectiveness.

Action and Intention is the dynamic duo behind any life-altering precept. The link between think and do is the basis of the popular Law of Attraction principle and healing modalities such as Emotional Freedom Technique (EFT).

Similarly, the importance of implementing Action and Intention is the foundation of all major religions.

Jesus taught: "What good is it, my brothers, if someone says he has faith but does not have works? So also faith by itself, if it does not have works, is dead" (James 2:14-17).

The Quran reads: "All actions are judged by motives, and each person will be rewarded according to their intention."

Reflect on the Buddha's sage words: "An idea that is developed and put into action is more important than an idea that exists only as an idea."

The relationship between Action and Intention is not only touted by spiritualists, but also by scientists. Researchers have been debating the causal relationship between the two ever since neuroscientist Benjammin Libet conducted a groundbreaking study on free will and action in the 1980s. Libet's study provided evidence that our brains initiate voluntary movements before we are even aware that we have decided to move. Whether Intention causes Action, or Action causes Intention, the mutually beneficial relationship between the two is undeniable.

Action unmotivated by a reason or goal produces empty and unful-filled results. Likewise, Intention without Action will simply remain an unmanifested thought. While feng shui can produce results without Intention, the results will manifest to a far greater degree with a little bit of mental focus and determination.

## You Are Already a Feng Shui Master!

Or you can be, if you just strengthen that muscle known as intu-ition…or *awareness*.

Have you ever walked into a clutter-filled home and immediately felt claustrophobic? Perhaps you even experienced physical symptoms, such as constricted breath.

Does the sight of your neighbor's overgrown, junk-filled front lawn fill you with such frustration that you find yourself entering and exit-ing your home via the back door in order to avoid the eyesore?

Most of us have a natural awareness of what makes us uncomfortable. Sometimes we can literally feel the chi suffocating. While many of us sense it wouldn't be ideal to live across from a cemetery (if that doesn't make you uncomfortable then practice flexing that intuition muscle!) everyone's chi monitor varies. Some people may enjoy living close to a school. The early hours and sounds of playing children stimulate and enliven their chi. Others may find the sounds of the recess bells and the children's shouts of glee to be jarring.

Feng shui may tell you the best location for your bed, but you might just sleep more soundly in a non-ideal spot. And that is okay! This book is designed to help you increase your awareness, but ultimately you are your own chi-guide.

*Feng Shui on a Dime* encourages you to start tapping into your inner feng shui consultant. Be aware of the space around you. How do crowds affect you? What vegetation and landscapes calm you? What kind of weather do you enjoy the most? What colors stimulate you and what colors make you feel anxious?

As you make the situational changes recommended in this book, notice how your life changes, notice how your chi changes, and notice how the people around you are influenced by the balance and harmonious energy that surrounds every aspect of your life.

# Chapter One

# YOUR HEALTH

Without health, it is difficult to appreciate the fullness of other areas of your life. What good is a new romance or a fabulous family if you cannot enjoy them because you feel too ill? What good is all the money in the world if you cannot spend it on vacations because your body isn't fit enough to travel? Aligning our health is the key to aligning other ill-fitting areas of our lives.

The good news is that we are powerful enough to influence energy in order to improve both physical and mental health.

This chapter investigates common arrangement issues and how they may ("may" being the operative word here) be impacting your health. Use the recommended solutions to realign your space according to feng shui principles, but don't stress out if your bed is under a beam and you're worried it's going to cause migraines. If you find a link between misplaced furniture and a health condition you're currently facing, then try out the solution (being sure to set it with Intention), but certainly don't diagnose a health problem or let a less-than-ideal setup stress you out. As with everything in life, take the suggested arrangements in this chapter with stride and balance. Experiment with a little at a time so that you don't get overwhelmed and you can better assess what solutions are working for you.

*Note: None of the feng shui cures in this book are intended to replace medical advice, or to diagnose, prescribe or treat any disease, condition, illness or injury. If you have, or suspect you have, a health ailment, it is imperative that you consult a licensed physician.*

## The Kitchen

Let's start with the area of the home that influences health the most: the kitchen. It makes perfect sense, doesn't it? The kitchen is the nucleus of the home; the place where you feed your body the sustenance it needs to keep you strong, healthy and vital. A kitchen in disarray may be contributing to a body in disarray and be negatively impacting your health.

Let's take a look at an archetypal feng shui kitchen. Don't worry if the anatomy of your kitchen isn't a match. No need to go breaking and resetting bones—a simple facelift in the form of non-invasive surgery is all it really needs!

**Check the boxes that describe your kitchen.**

❑ The kitchen is located in the back half of your home.

Such placement encourages serenity and security, and protects the stove's vulnerable energies. The stove is especially important because it generates, stores and manages chi.

❑ The stove is positioned so that it is not directly across from a door. We don't want that energy escaping!

❑ The stove, sink and refrigerator form a triangle and sit 6 to 8 feet apart from each other.

❑ The stove is placed away from the kitchen's main pathway to protect healthy chi.

- [ ] The stove (especially the top) is free of dirt and grime.

- [ ] The entire kitchen is clean and clutter free. Knives and unused appliances are tucked away safe and sound in the cupboards.

- [ ] The stove is either against a wall (but not jammed in a corner) or in the center of the kitchen.

> Feng shui experts differ as to the best location. Some say a stove placed against a wall is beneficial because it promotes physical and mental stability. Others recommend a stove in the center of the kitchen because it provides a commanding view of the room and the doorway.

- [ ] The kitchen only has one door—the kitchen door!

- [ ] Bright and clean, the kitchen is decorated in light colors.

> White is the most preferable because it signifies purity and cleanliness and can also help promote weight loss.

The perfect feng shui kitchen is hard to come by, unless of course you've designed it from scratch. Chances are you didn't check all the boxes. Fortunately, there are easy adjustments you can make to remedy any feng-shui no-nos.

Let's take a look at some less-than-ideal kitchen setups and the health issues they may be impacting.

*Kitchen in Center of House*

A kitchen located in the center of the home too intensely affects our chi. The kitchen contains an abundant amount of energy; there is a constant flow, as family members move in and out of the kitchen throughout the day. This intensity is stimulated further by the energy radiating from the stove and electrical appliances.

The center of the home is connected to the heart and stomach, and such over-stimulating energy can adversely affect the **digestive system** and **heart health**, as well as contribute to **emotional instability** and **moodiness**. Symptoms such as *high blood pressure, heartburn* and *constipation* may develop.

*Feng Shui Solution:*

- To neutralize the energy of a central kitchen decorate with earth tones, which have a calming and grounding effect. **Yellow is recommended, as the color aids digestion.** A pair of yellow curtains or a wash of yellow on the walls will do the trick. Add a yellow potted vase or some yellow daisies for a simple and cheap cure that can have a dramatic effect on your health.
- Using earth elements to help balance your health is also a worthwhile technique. Add stone and ceramic accessories to your kitchen, such as a ceramic cookie jar or a wall clock made of stone.

*Kitchen at Front Door*

If your front door leads straight into your kitchen (a likely setup for

apartment dwellers) you may be experiencing **digestive problems,**
unexplained **weight gain** and **eating disorders,** such as *binge eating.*
It's easy to have food on the brain and hard to stay away from it
when the first thing you see upon entering your home is the fridge.

---

*Feng Shui Solution:*

♦ Hang a wind chime or a faceted crystal ball prism over the
  stove, directly above the cook.

---

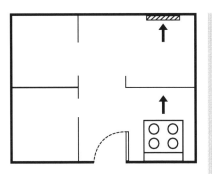

♦ To help diffuse the intensity
  and to pull the energy away
  from the kitchen, hang a
  large mirror in the back of
  the house, directly in line
  with the stove.

*Stove Visible from Front Door*

Perhaps you do not immediately enter your kitchen from the front
door, but can see still see the stove upon entering. Similar **weight-re-
lated** and **digestive health problems** may prevail.

*Feng Shui Solution:*

- The best fix is to block the front door view of the kitchen with a curtain or screen. Get funky with beads, bamboo blinds, a decorative bookshelf or hanging lights.
- If you have an open floor plan and blocking the view isn't an option, then draw the focus elsewhere with a piece of art or a fountain (even a small table fountain will do).
- For a traditional cure, place two brass wind chimes or two hanging crystals along the path between the front door and the stove to diffuse the negative effects and disperse energy.

*Kitchen Door Directly in Line with Bedroom Door*

That fiery, vibrant chi from the kitchen escapes into the calm sanctity of the bedroom, adversely affecting your health as you sleep. **Chronic health conditions** may develop over time.

*Feng Shui Solution:*

- Keep the kitchen door closed.

*Kitchen Door Directly in Line with Front or Back Doors*

When a kitchen sits in the direct path of a front or back door the healthy chi too easily escapes. Various illnesses can arise according to an individual's predisposition, and may eventually contribute to more **chronic conditions** such as *diabetes* and *heart disease*. Such placement is also thought to promote *alcoholism*.

*Feng Shui Solution:*

♦ Hang a mirror on the front or back doors to reflect and contain the positive energy.
♦ A plant or flower on a table next to the front or back door can also work wonders in keeping positive energy in the home.

*Multiple Doors in Kitchen*

Too many doors create too much energy entering and exiting the kitchen, which may be contributing to **anxiety**, and **mental** and **physical imbalance**.

*Feng Shui Solution:*

♦ An overall and highly effective cure for any kitchen issue is to hang a faceted crystal ball in the center of the kitchen. Traditional feng shui recommends hanging the crystal from a red ribbon, cut to a 9-inch increment. Red signifies fire and is thought to deliver the most powerful transformative effects. Nine-inch increments, such as 9, 18 or 27 inches, are important because 9 is considered the most potent number, symbolizing completion and accomplishment.

*Feng Shui on a Dime* recommends checking in with your inner feng shui consultant. If you feel better using a color or material that melds with your décor then have at it. It is the Intention behind the cures that generates the strongest result.

*Kitchen Next to Bathroom*

This is a common scenario in both apartments and homes. It just makes good design sense to keep the plumbing in one central area, which means kitchens often sit next to, or lie back-to-back with, bathrooms. Not the most ideal setup according to feng shui, but one that is easily neutralized.

If your bathroom and kitchen sink share a wall and are positioned back-to-back, the arrangement does not need fixing. When the toilet, bathtub or kitchen sink lies back-to-back with the stove, **digestive** or **urinary tract issues** may arise.

*Feng Shui Solution:*

♦ Hang a mirror behind the stove with the reflective surface facing out toward the stove. The mirror should be the same width as the stove and reach to the top of the stove.

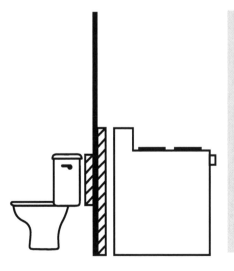

♦ A mirror on both sides of the shared wall intensifies the cure. Place a convex mirror behind the toilet with the reflective surface facing out towards the bathroom. This keeps the draining energy of the toilet out of your kitchen and where it belongs.

> - If you are all mirrored out, paint both sides of the wall a shade of green, any hue will do. Green represents energy and vitality and helps stimulate the wood element, which is especially important to health.

*Stove and Bed Share a Wall*

If the stove shares a wall back-to-back with a bed, health problems may occur. **Mental health** is particularly affected; common ailments include *insomnia, restlessness* and *agitation*.

*Feng Shui Solution:*

- The suggested cure is to move the bed so that it does not lie back-to-back with the stove.
- Unlike the stove/toilet cure, **it is not advisable to hang a mirror above the bed or facing the bed**. Such placement not only deprives you of sound sleep, but is also thought to influence **heart conditions**. If you have mirrors in these positions, place them elsewhere in the bedroom so that they do not reflect the bed.

*Bed Located Directly over Stove*

When a bed lies directly above the stove you may experience **fatigue** and **irritability**. *Cancer* and *tumors* in the area of the body directly above the stove may also be an issue. **Heart** and **blood pressure problems** may be exacerbated.

*Feng Shui Solution:*

- Move the bed.
- If moving the bed is not an option, then strengthen its foundation by grounding it with the earth element. Place a rug infused with earth tones under your bed, or purchase earth-toned linens and pillows.
- Another option is to place a small round mirror, shiny side down, underneath the bed in order to diffuse the fire energy of the stove.

*Toilet Located Directly over Stove*

The routine flushing of the toilet sucks the life energy from the stove, and may leave you **feeling drained** with a **weakened immune system**.

*Feng Shui Solution:*

- Place a small round mirror above the stove, directly underneath the toilet with the mirror side facing down.

*Stove Sits Directly Across from Sink*

Many feng shui experts believe it is best if your stove does not lie directly across from or next to a sink. The stove represents Fire and the sink represents Water; two opposing elements too nearby create conflict. If you feel the direct opposition of the two does indeed create conflicting energy in your home, then implement the following feng shui remedy.

There is a more practical explanation for this symbolism: in ancient China, people cooked over an open flame, so it made sense to avoid a layout that placed Fire and Water too close. If the energy between the stove and sink does not bother you, then consider the practical explanation and forego a cure.

*Feng Shui Solution:*

- Place something green, such as a healthy plant or a green rug, between the stove and sink. This solution also applies if the sink is adjacent to the stove.
- Another option is to place a 1-inch square mirror on the door of the stove.

Square and rectangular mirrors promote balance.

*Stove Sits Too Close to Refrigerator*

The hot energy of the stove and the cold energy of the fridge just don't mix. Conflict can translate to health problems.

*Feng Shui Solution:*

- On the side of the refrigerator that faces the stove, strategically place a mirror.
- Hang a wind chime or crystal between the fridge and the stove to balance the conflicting energies.
- You can also separate the energy by placing a potted plant between the two.

Inviting in the earth element in the form of stone and ceramic, and the wood element in the form of a green plant, revitalizes chi in any kitchen.

*Stove Underneath Window*

When a window sits directly above a stove—especially if bars frame the window—***anemia*** and other **blood disorders** may result.

*Feng Shui Solution:*

- Add the color green. One option is to wrap ivy around the bars. Adding green curtains or an odd number of healthy green potted plants to the windowsill works just as well.

Odd numbers are considered auspicious in feng shui.

*Outside Door in Kitchen*

Outside doors that lead into the kitchen, especially garage doors, can compromise your health. Exhaust fumes and environmental toxins can too easily mix with your food.

*Feng Shui Solution:*

- Use the outside door less.

- Hang a flute horizontally above the outside door. A bamboo flute slows flow of chi so it does not rapidly escape from the door. Flutes also offer protection and a feeling of peace.

*Kitchen Door Not Visible Behind You*

You need to be able to see the kitchen entrance when you are cooking at the stove in order to feel safe and calm. When the kitchen door is not visible it can affect your **psyche** and **nervous system**, the health of which is extremely important to your overall well-being.

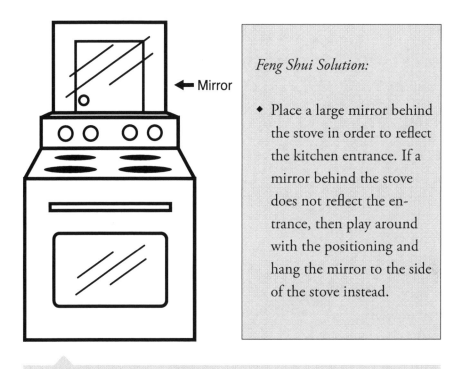

*Feng Shui Solution:*

* Place a large mirror behind
  the stove in order to reflect
  the kitchen entrance. If a
  mirror behind the stove
  does not reflect the entrance, then play around
  with the positioning and
  hang the mirror to the side
  of the stove instead.

Stainless steel utensils also have a reflecting aspect and can be used
to create more space and a sense of safety. Mirrors behind stoves
can entail quite a bit of upkeep, so getting creative with reflective
kitchen accessories may be a more practical solution for you.

*Microwave Above Stove*

Although ideal for space efficiency, a microwave above the stove is not
ideal for health. A microwave stunts the flow of energy through the
stove, and subsequently through our entire bodies. Not to mention,
microwaves emit radiation and have been shown to increase the prev-
alence of **cancer cells** in the body, **lower the immune system** and
**decrease hormone production**.

> *Feng Shui Solution:*
>
> * Move the microwave to a countertop away from the stove, or remove the microwave from the kitchen altogether.

Hanging a faceted crystal prism or a metal wind chime over the stove is also a terrific overall kitchen cure, especially if stove placement is an issue.

## The Bedroom

Having tackled the kitchen—the area of the home most influential to overall health—let's move to the master bedroom, where your body goes to rest, recuperate and rejuvenate.

Let's take a look at some bedroom mishaps that may be negatively affecting your health, dealing first with those that **disrupt your sleep**.

*Bedroom Too Close to Front Door*

A master bedroom located too close to a front door can trigger **insomnia** and **restless sleep**.

> The ideal location for a master bedroom is in the back of the house, diagonally opposite to the entrance.

*Feng Shui Solution:*

- If possible, move the master suite to a room located farther in the back of the house, as far from the front door as possible.

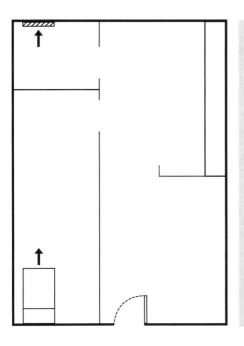

- If a change of location is not possible, position a large mirror at the back of the house, directly in line with your bed. Such an arrangement will energetically pull the bed to the rear of the house, thereby encouraging deeper sleep. For best results, the top of the mirror should be higher than the crown of the tallest sleeper's head.

*Irregularly Shaped Bedroom*

An oddly shaped bedroom may also lead to **insomnia**. No need to remodel; try one of the following solutions.

Rectangular or square-shaped bedrooms are the most auspicious.

---

*Feng Shui Solution:*

+ Hang a crystal from the center of the bedroom.
+ Use a room divider screen to balance the room's shape.
+ Balance out the irregular angles with lush plants in the appropriate corners.
+ Decorate with a rectangular or square area rug.

---

*A Towering Headboard*

A headboard made of built-in bookshelves, or one that towers over the bed, can also cause **insomnia** and **restlessness**, partly because it is oppressive, and partly because it can hamper progress.

---

*Feng Shui Solution:*

+ To encourage calmness and relaxation, replace the headboard with a strong solid headboard made of either wood or fabric. The headboard should be firmly attached to the bed frame and should not feature rods or split wood in the middle, as such designs trigger a sense of imbalance.

---

*Bed in Direct Line with the Door*

When the bed lies in the direct path of the door, **health issues**, as well as **disrupted sleep**, may arise. *The body parts that are the most affected are those that lay in the energetic path of the door*. For example, if the energy travels directly across your stomach, you may suffer from digestive problems.

There is also a bit of ancient symbolism in this bed placement. The Chinese believe sleeping with your feet pointing out the door is bad for your health, because when a person dies, they are carried out feet first.

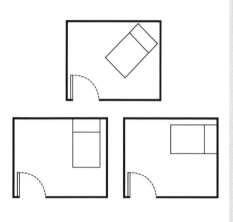

The bed is best placed in the "command position," which is diagonally farthest from the door. This allows you to benefit from the free-flowing chi entering your bedroom without being bombarded by its strong energy. It also gives you visual command of the room, which promotes a sense of peace, relaxation and stability.

*Feng Shui Solution:*

* Move your bed away from the door's path.
* If changing the location of your bed is not an option, place a table or nightstand between the door and the bed. A medium-sized plant on top of the table will also help defend against the intense energy.

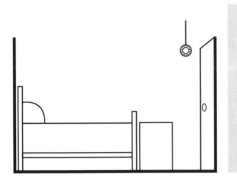

You can also block the energy of the door with an upholstered bench or chaise lounge at the foot of the bed.

* You can also block the energy of the door with an upholstered bench or chaise lounge at the foot of the bed.
* Hang a crystal over the door.

*Bed Underneath Window*

Those **fitful nights of sleep** could be due to chi flying out the window above your head. Windows drain energy, and too many windows in a bedroom, especially if right above your bed, can rob you of sleep and leave you feeling exhausted in the morning, even if you did catch the appropriate amount of zzzzzs.

*Feng Shui Solution:*

* Reposition the bed away from the windows.
* If a change of location is not possible, make sure your bed has a strong and solid headboard, which is imperative regardless of bed position.
* Opt for heavy draperies (like blackout curtains) to create the illusion of a strong solid wall behind you.

*Mirror Across from Bed*

A mirror that is positioned directly across from the bed may cause a **restless night's sleep**, or frequent **insomnia**. Reflective surfaces bounce back your worries, keeping you tossing and turning throughout the night.

There is an ancient belief that when you sleep, your soul travels, but if it sees itself in the mirror it may get freaked out and leave for good.

*Feng Shui Solution:*

- Reposition the mirror. If the mirror is attached to a piece of furniture, angle the mirror so that it is not directly facing the bed.
- If the mirror is part of a dresser, you can deflect the negative impact with crystal perfume bottles (or crystals themselves) lined up in front. You can also get creative and hide the mirror with a stack of books, a potted plant or a decorative piece of art.
- Hang a crystal over the front of the mirror by attaching the string to the back of the dresser.
- Cover the mirror with a light fabric before you go to sleep.
- If the mirror is a closet door, then hang a curtain that you can draw closed at night.

*Heavy Furniture*

Tall, heavy furniture is overpowering and can **disrupt sleep** and **health**.

*Feng Shui Solution:*

- Neutralize the effects by raising the bed a bit so that the height is equalized.
- Buy some new furniture with your tax refund perhaps?

*Clutter Under the Bed*

Be it clutter or storage, the area underneath the bed should be kept clear. **Sleep patterns** may be **negatively affected** otherwise. When the chi underneath you is able to circulate freely, the chi in your body is able to circulate more freely as well.

*Feng Shui Solution:*

* Remove objects from under the bed.
* If you live in a small space and you need the extra storage, then pack things neatly into boxes or plastic storage bins. Make sure objects are not crammed under the bed, but lie neatly underneath and can be accessed easily.

*Electronics in the Bedroom*

Due to size and space constrictions, our bedrooms often become multipurpose rooms. You may have your home office in a corner of your bedroom. And almost everyone has a TV in the bedroom these days. Electronics, such as computers, televisions, printers, stereos, telephones, etc., promise to **keep you awake** and **restless** at night.

*Feng Shui Solution:*

* Remove all electronics.
* If you must have your home office in your bedroom, separate it from your sleeping space with a folding screen. You can also separate your bed from your desk by hanging curtains from the ceiling.
* If you insist on having a TV in the bedroom, then keep it in an armoire or cabinet when you are not using it. The good thing about flat screen TVs is that when they are off they aren't reflective, so they are less troublesome than mirrors across from the bed.

**Feng Shui Tips for Restful Sleep**

Optimal health begins with sound sleep. Here are some suggestions to ensure a good night's rest:

* Place dried lavender and chamomile herbs in a bowl next to your bed. Or diffuse essential oils in an aromatherapy diffuser. These herbs have been used throughout the ages as natural sleep aids.
* Add more plants to your bedroom to increase oxygen and help you relax.
* Remove papers, bills and calendars (or keep them hidden behind a decorative screen in your bedroom's designated office space) so that your day-to-day affairs don't follow you into the bed and into your dreams.
* Keep the night in with heavy drapery that shuts out the light.
* Decorate with restful images to encourage sound sleep, such as scenes of nature and quiet interiors.

A bedroom that follows good feng shui principles helps keep ailments at bay, whereas a bedroom that falls prey to bad feng shui can exacerbate health issues. We are all predisposed to certain health conditions according to lifestyle and genetics, but a predisposition isn't a diagnosis. You can use feng shui to help turn the right genes on and disease-promoting genes off! Take a look at some common arrangements that may be impacting your health.

*Ceiling Fan over Bed*

A ceiling fan over the bed may help on those sticky, summer nights, but many feng shui experts will tell you it is causing more harm than good. A fan directly over the bed disrupts the flow of energy and can cause **physical** and **emotional turmoil**. A fan directly above your head when you sleep may cause *sinus problems*; if positioned over the heart, *heart conditions* may arise; and if positioned over the stomach, *digestive problems* may thrive.

> *Feng Shui Solution:*
>
> - Retire the ceiling fan and hang a crystal from it while you're at it.
> - You can also create a canopy using a soft, natural fabric to cover the ceiling fan and offer protection. It adds a little romance to the bedroom, which never hurts!

*Beam over Bed*

A beam over the bed is constrictive and oppressive and can lead to **heart conditions**. It may also *affect whatever part of the body it sits above*. For instance, if it runs along the foot of the bed you may experience ankle pain, whereas if it runs above your pillow, you may be prone to migraines. Paint the beam the same color as the ceiling (preferably white) before implementing any of the following cures.

*Feng Shui Solution:*

- Buy a canopy bed, or create a canopy using lightweight, natural fabric such as linen.
- You can also soften the impact of beams by hanging decorative lanterns or other decorative symbols from the beams (just not over the bed).

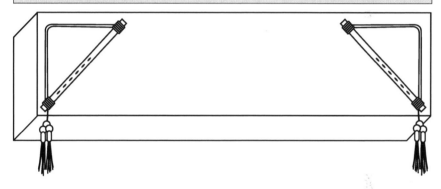

- Traditional cure: Hang bamboo flutes on both ends of the beam. The flutes should hang at 45-degree angles. Do not hang the flutes or any other heavy object over your bed.

*Bathroom Door in Bedroom*

A bathroom door in the bedroom, while convenient, **drains energy** and can deteriorate health. You should not be able to see the toilet from the bed; such a view can lead to **stomach** or **intestinal issues**.

*Feng Shui Solution:*

- To counteract the negative effects, hang a full-length mirror on the outside of the bathroom door and keep the bathroom door closed.
- Strengthen the bedroom door and weaken the bathroom door with color. Use grounding bold color for the outside of the door facing the bedroom.
- Ground the energy of the bathroom by placing a small bowl of rocks or crystals above the toilet.
- Place two plants on either side of the door to balance the energy.

*Fireplace in Bedroom*

A fireplace in the bedroom is extremely romantic, but also draining. **Exhaustion** and **stress** are common symptoms.

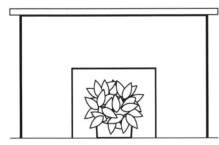

*Feng Shui Solution:*

- Refrain from using, and place a potted plant in front of the opening.

*Sharp Corners in Bedroom*

Take a look around your bedroom. Do you see any sharp arrows pointing toward your bed? These arrows can come from angular furniture, such as a chest of drawers or a nearby nightstand, or the energy can be pointing at you from the corner of a protruding wall. The goal is to neutralize the sharp energy so that it does not negatively impact your health.

> *Feng Shui Solution:*
>
> * Reposition furniture so that it is not pointing directly at your bed.
> * Place a plant in front of any sharply protruding corners. For instance, place a tall plant in front of a sharply angled wall, or a medium-sized plant at the corner of a nightstand.
> * Plants can also be hung in front of an angled corner.
> * Drape a piece of fabric over furniture to soften the sharp edges.

**Bedroom Panaceas for Overall Health**

* If you want to enhance your health, redecorate with the color green, which fosters health, vitality, longevity, growth and rebirth.
* If you go through mental and emotional imbalances, try decorating with blue, which promotes relaxation, calmness and inner peace.
* Keep the air clean with an air purifier. Open the windows on occasion to generate chi and help air circulate.

**Looking to Get Pregnant?**

The bedroom will require some adjustments. Take advantage of the following tips:

* While there should not be any clutter underneath the bed, do not clean under the bed.

The soul of the unborn baby is said to visit its mother-to-be. Cleaning under the bed may frighten the baby away.

- If already pregnant, do not add furniture; likewise because you do not want to scare the baby away.
- If there is a ceiling fan above the bed, remove it, or neutralize the cutting energy by hanging a crystal from it.
- Don't move the bed if you are looking to conceive.
- Pomegranates and elephants are symbols of fertility, so add these images to your décor. Some images of babies thrown into the mix wouldn't hurt either. If you feel connected to another fertility symbol, by all means, use that!

## The Bathroom

When we consider all that goes down in the bathroom—the double entendre is intentional—it is easy to understand its influence on our health.

The location of the bathroom has the most dramatic effect on our health.

### Toilet in Center of Home

Toilets should not be located in the center of the house. The water element is thought to cause **depression**, **colds** and **diarrhea**. To counteract the draining pull on our vital energy, try one of the following solutions.

*Feng Shui Solution:*

- Paint the walls red and decorate with candles to spark more fire energy.
- Add an earth element to the décor, such as a ceramic or stone vase or candleholder to help balance the energy.
- Make sure the bathroom light is bright.
- A wonderful and easy remedy is to affix a mirror to the outside of the bathroom door to keep the healthy chi from draining away.

You don't want to flush away all that good energy.

**Bathroom Cures**

Here are tips to help keep healthy chi circulating throughout your bathroom and the rest of your home.

- Add plants and flowers to your bathroom to stimulate chi.
- Keep the toilet seat down when not in use.
- Keep shower and sink drains plugged when not in use.
- Keep the bathroom door closed at all times.
- Place a crystal on the toilet tank to help balance the chi.
- Windows are important for ventilation.
- Make sure the plumbing is in good working order.
- Get rid of all expired medicine and toiletries.
- Keep first aid essentials tucked away so you are not reminded of possible emergencies and accidents.

## The Dining Room

The arrangement of the dining room contributes greatly to your overall health, especially **digestive health**. There are a few adjustments you can make to your dining room to positively enhance health.

*Dining Room at Front Door*

A front door leading into the dining room can encourage **poor eating habits** and **drain energy levels**.

*Feng Shui Solution:*

♦ Hang a crystal over the center of the table or invest in a centerpiece made of crystal/semi-precious stones. This also is a great cure if you have two entryways into your dining room that are directly opposite each other. It slows the flow of energy, allowing it to circulate through the room and soothe your digestive system. Your eating habits should also improve.

*Stove Visible from Dining Room Table*

A stove in sight while eating may lead to **overeating**, or another type of eating disorder.

*Feng Shui Solution:*

+ Keep a bowl full of fresh oranges in the center of the table.
+ You can also separate this view with a beaded curtain or decorative drapes.
+ Traditional cure: to create a sense of peace and calm hang two bamboo flutes at 45-degree angles over the kitchen door.

*Cramped and Cluttered Dining Space*

Ideally, four walls surround the dining table in order to minimize distraction and aid in digestion. A dining room that is too cramped with furniture can impede proper digestion. Likewise, a dining table that is too big for the room can restrict digestion.

*Feng Shui Solution:*

+ Eliminate the amount of furniture in the dining room.
+ Purchase a dining table that is proportional in size to the dining room.
+ Keep the table free of clutter, including work and school projects. Remember, the dining room is for "dining" and the focal point should always be the table.

## Dining Room Tips and Tricks for Optimal Health

* The color blue helps stimulate weight loss by decreasing appetite and helping to reduce blood pressure. Add blue placemats or blue napkins, but remember to set an Intention!
* Earth tone colors, such as yellow, coffee and taupe, are wonderful

color choices for dining rooms.

- Give yourself and your family time away from the outside world. Shut off your cell phones when you are eating and concentrate on providing your body with healthy nourishing foods.

## The Exterior

Many people focus only on the inside of their homes, not realizing that the outside environment—from the neighborhood and street, to the driveway, yard, walkway and porch—is equally important. Think of it this way: You give directions to someone coming to your home for the first time so they don't get lost. In the same way, you must give the chi directions or it won't ever make it inside.

You want to create a welcoming environment outside, full of refreshing, vibrant energy that is not too frenetic or stationary. If you live on a street that has no activity, the energy surrounding your home is too stagnant and your **physical** and **mental energy may suffer** as a result. Balance is imperative, as too much intensity also robs you of essential energy, as is the case on a street that is too busy with traffic. Health problems may ensue when your chi becomes blocked.

Plant trees and use water cures to create and tame movement.

Beware of the following misplacements.

*Y or T-intersection*

When the street ends at your front yard, your home is bombarded with energy that is moving much too fast, thereby promoting **paranoia, depression, illness** and unfortunate **accidents**.

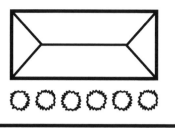

*Cul-de-sac*

*Feng Shui Solution:*

- Cut the intense energy in half by planting hedges or building a fence over the front line of your yard.

- Hang a wind chime over the front door to minimize the impact.

- A traditional, inexpensive, but very potent and recommended cure is to hang a Ba-Gua mirror above the front door. This octagon-shaped, wooden mirror is usually only 4 to 6 inches wide and colored red and green, but modern versions work as well, especially when set with focused Intention.

If your home lies at the end of a cul-de-sac you may be suffering from stagnant energy. Your **lower body** is particularly vulnerable.

*Feng Shui Solution:*

- A water cure is the best solution, as moving water enlivens energy. Place a fountain with an upward spray at the center of the yard, the beginning of the driveway or near the front door.
- A cheaper alternative is to hang a bird feeder near the front door to help attract and revitalize dead energy. A hummingbird feeder equals less mess!
- Make sure that all outside fixtures work and that there is no clutter or debris blocking the flow of energy. That means no empty plastic water bottles or grime-filled BBQs.

**Tips to Keep Healthy Chi Circulating Outside**

- The color green promotes hope, growth and oxygen, three ingredients for a sound mind and body. Revitalizing your yard with trees and plants, especially flower and fruit-bearing trees, helps the energy in your environment and your body circulate freely. Keep the energy flowing up and out by planting upward, rather than downward sloping trees.

Avoid planting mulberry trees, which symbolize death. Barren trees need to be either tended to or removed, as they can lead to failing health and a disturbed psyche.

- Decorate the outside of your property with earth tones, such as yellow and orange, which help to improve overall health and well-being.
- A very simple fix that can stimulate both health and money is to paint your front door green.

# The Entrance

First impressions are important and the entryway into your home should support abundance and vigor. Ideally, your front door should open onto a large, unobstructed entryway.

*Split View*

If your view upon entering your home is split by a wall, you may suffer from **anxiety, stress** or other ***psychological issues***.

> *Feng Shui Solution:*
>
> ◆ Place a large mirror on the wall that partially blocks your view. It will open up the space and create a sense of peace and balance.

*Front Door in Line with Window*

If your front door is directly in line with a window, the healthy chi can too easily escape!

> *Feng Shui Solution:*
>
> ◆ Slow down and contain the chi by adding a plant in front of the window, or between the window and the door.

# Household Fixtures

*Angled Doors*

Straight doors promote balanced energy, but angled doors can trigger **emotional imbalances** and lead to **spinal, bone** and **joint** problems. It is especially important to avoid angled doors leading into the master bedroom or the office.

*Feng Shui Solution:*

- Hang a metal chime on the inside and the outside of the door.
- Hang a crystal on the inside and the outside of the door.
- For a less traditional, but more practical and highly effective cure, draw attention to the wall right next to the angled door. You can suggest a strong focal point by painting the adjacent wall a bold color, or adding a tall plant if the space allows.

*Skylights*

Skylights are linked to problems with the **back of the body** and the **head**. Feng shui experts advise against adding a skylight to an existing structure, as it can lead to future **accidents** or **surgeries**. The worst locations for a skylight are at the entrance to the home, in the center of the home, or in the kitchen or master bedroom.

A skylight over the bed is a threat to the sleeper and can affect overall well-being.

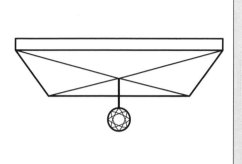

<table>
<tr><td>

*Feng Shui Solution:*

♦ Hang a crystal from the skylight to neutralize the effects.
♦ You can also add a canopy of softly draped fabric above the bed.

</td></tr>
</table>

*Irregular Ceilings*

If ceilings are multilevel, slanted or uneven, **confusion, mental instability, moodiness, high blood pressure** or **imbalanced blood sugar levels** may be an issue.

*Feng Shui Solution:*

♦ Hang chandeliers or crystals, or drape fabrics to balance the ceiling.

**Mental/physical health** is especially affected if you are sleeping under an angled ceiling.

*Feng Shui Solution:*

♦ Hang a crystal over the head of the bed.
♦ Place a light that shines up toward the ceiling.
♦ Hang plants vertically under the slant.
♦ Don't forget the canopy trick!

# Favorite Cures

Let's take a more in-depth look at some of the health-replenishing cures mentioned throughout this chapter.

### Mirrors

We've seen how mirrors can be used to deflect, direct and contain energy. The typical rule of thumb is the larger the mirror, the more effective the cure. Don't let broken or chipped mirrors slip by your notice. Mirrors that are broken or distorted can have a harmful effect on your **mental health**.

### Plants

Plants should be healthy, green and vibrant. Dead, wilting plants can lead to stagnant chi and physical ailments. Are you a fan of dried flowers, wreaths and potpourri? Even the most beautifully arranged dried flowers are still quite literally "dead flowers." Rather than keeping dried arrangements, buy fresh flowers weekly, being sure to replace them at the first sign of wilting, or invest in artificial plants that'd fool even the greenest of thumbs.

### Fish

Fish are wonderful cures if you are looking to fortify your mental health. Water is a natural **mood stabilizer**. Be sure to keep the fish healthy and the water clean, and replace the fish immediately when they die.

A very simple and easy fish to care for is a beta fish. When kept in a large bowl with pebbles, algae and fun décor, and fed twice a day, a healthy beta can live three to four years or more!

## Water

Water is a wonderful, refreshing cure. Not only does it stimulate stagnant chi, but it also releases negative ions into the environment.

Negative ions are important because they help purify and freshen the air, literally sweeping away the pollens, toxins and pollution.

## Mobile

If you are looking to **revive circulation** and **energy**, mobile cures, such as windsocks, flags, banners, pinwheels and whirligigs, are wonderful remedies.

## Rock

Earth elements, such as rocks, encourage a feeling of groundedness and peacefulness, and are especially important if you are looking to **balance your moods** and calm **anxiety**. For instance, if your home is L-shaped and missing a life area from the Ba-Gua Map (page 61), you can fill it in with a healing and grounding rock garden. Rocks cost virtually nothing! Be sure to set your Intention as you collect your rocks.

## Fragrance

Essential oils and incense act as mood and health enhancers. You can improve your living space by using essential oils as room fresheners. Put a few drops in an aromatherapy diffuser or lamp scent ring, or simply add 10 drops to 2 cups of boiling water and breathe in the benefits. You can even add a few drops to your laundry wash and trash cans!

### The Top Essential Oils for Health

*Pine* treats…

- Psoriasis
- Eczema
- Pimples
- Food poisoning
- Joint pain
- Arthritis
- Respiratory issues
- Low metabolism

*Lemon Balm* is a wonderful…

- Antidepressant
- Anxiety reducer
- Anti-inflammatory agent
- Sleep aid

It helps heal…

- Ulcers
- Bacterial infections
- Headaches
- High blood pressure

*Sandalwood* promotes mental health by…

- Raising self-esteem
- Eliminating insecurity
- Reducing stress
- Combating depression

Sandalwood promotes physical health by…

- Supporting the female reproductive system and endocrine health
- Encouraging deep sleep
- Preventing and healing urinary tract infections
- Curing bronchitis and laryngitis
- Improving the appearance of stretch marks
- Promoting healthy looking skin

*Frankincense* treats…

- Lack of confidence
- Grief
- Weakened immune system
- Cancer
- Depression, anxiety and panic attacks
- Allergies
- Herpes
- Headaches
- Head traumas
- Asthma
- Bronchitis
- Coughing
- Scars
- Stretch marks

**Cedarwood** is a wonderful aid for...

- Anxiety and stress
- Skin conditions such as psoriasis, dandruff and dermatitis
- Cough
- Bronchitis
- Hair loss
- Tuberculosis
- Gonorrhea

**Rosemary** helps...

- Relieve aches and pains
- Soothe digestive issues
- Sharpen memory
- Ease respiratory illness
- Alleviate headaches
- Reduce stress
- Boost the immune system
- Treat the flu
- Balance skin

**Peppermint** soothes...

- Nausea
- Stomach problems
- Itching
- Sore muscles
- Headaches
- Symptoms of PMS

It can also help you concentrate!

**Lavender** is a natural...

- Antibiotic
- Germ-buster
- Digestive aid
- Pain reliever
- Sleep inducer
- Anxiety reducer
- Blood pressure reducer
- Acne fighter

*Geranium* can be used to reduce...

- Inflammation
- PMS
- Acne
- Oiliness
- Scars
- Body odor
- Fine lines and wrinkles

Geranium also stimulates circulation!

*Clove* is a great remedy for...

- Headaches
- Tooth and gum pain
- Bad breath
- Sore muscles
- Bug bites
- Cuts and scrapes
- Sinus problems
- Stomachaches
- Stress

*Black Pepper* aids...

- Digestion
- Cramps
- Joint and muscle pain
- Arthritis
- Bacterial infections

*Sesame Oil* contains fatty acids that...

- Lower blood pressure
- Reduce stress
- Inhibit the growth of cancer cells

## The Elements

According to feng shui, everything is made up of five elements: Wood, Fire, Earth, Metal and Water. The placement of elements can either positively or negatively affect your health. When elements conflict with one another, your physical and mental health may be compromised.

### *Wood*

Wood is the most crucial element to health. Represented by the color green and associated with the liver, Wood stimulates growth and vitality. To benefit from the healthful nature of Wood, decorate with plants, flowers, wood furniture and plant-based fabrics such as cotton. If you prefer not to decorate with wood, hang some landscape art on the walls, and decorate in green and blue hues.

*Wood in the Center of the Home*

Wood in the center of the home is not conducive to health. If Wood is the prominent element in the center of your home, either remove the wood or counter its effects by adding more Earth to the center of the home.

> The element Earth should be placed in the center of the home to enhance overall health.

The earth element can be added by using earth tones, such as yellow and gold, and ceramic or stone pottery. You can also balance the negative effects of Wood by adding the element, Metal, which destroys Wood. Decorate with a metal sculpture or table, and add in the color white.

## Home Homeostasis

In order for our bodies to function optimally, our systems must all be in working order. An ill-functioning digestive system impacts our liver, lungs and heart, and weakened cardiovascular health leads to serious conditions such as heart attack, stroke and death.

Likewise, our house systems should be kept in top-notch shape. Be on top of any plumbing, electrical or gas issues. Install a high-quality water filter and invest in air purifiers to ensure fresh air.

Remember to breathe deeply and fully as the healthy chi circulates more freely through your newly feng-shuied home.

❖ *Chapter Two* ❖

# YOUR WEALTH

Whether you're looking to improve a dismal financial situation or to increase an already steady cash flow, the tips and tricks that follow can help put a little more cushion in your wallet.

## The Kitchen

Like health, wealth is significantly impacted by the setup of your kitchen. For an in-depth discussion of the ideal kitchen layout, refer to Chapter 1 (pages 13-14). Let's review the most important principles.

### Placement

Ideally, your kitchen should be placed in the back part of your home. For troubleshooting improperly placed kitchens, such as kitchens in the front of the house and the center of the house, see pages 15-16.

### Size

Size counts. The larger the kitchen, the bigger your bank account. But don't worry if your apartment-sized kitchen is anything but spacious. You can enlarge the space simply by adding mirrors!

Hanging a crystal from the center of the kitchen ceiling is another simple way to expand your space.

## Color

Decorate with light colors, especially white, to rev up your wealth-generating potential. Use incandescent instead of fluorescent light bulbs. Save the mood lighting for the bedroom…bright is best!

## The Stove

The stove is your home's energy furnace. The cook, the food and the fire come together to energetically support health and wealth. You can activate your money-making potential by maximizing the position of your stove.

The stove is best placed in the command position. You want to have a clear view of the kitchen door when you're cooking at the stove. In many homes, however, the stove faces a wall and the kitchen door lies to the side or behind the cook. The easiest way to cure an obstructed view is to hang a mirror on the wall behind the stove. The mirror should be as wide as the stove and reach from the top of the stove to the hood of the stove, or just above your head (see page 25). Use heat-tempered glass so that it can withstand the heat from the stove!

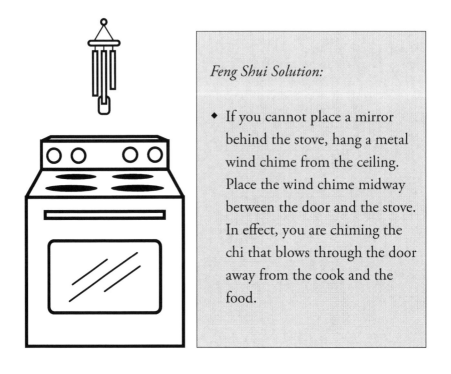

*Feng Shui Solution:*

♦ If you cannot place a mirror behind the stove, hang a metal wind chime from the ceiling. Place the wind chime midway between the door and the stove. In effect, you are chiming the chi that blows through the door away from the cook and the food.

Remember how the hot energy from the stove conflicts with the cold energy from the fridge? It doesn't just put a strain on your health; it impacts your finances as well! See the suggested cures on page 22.

**Cleanliness**

A dirty stove can leave you feeling depressed and fatigued, making it more difficult to make money. For a financial uplift, keep your stove free of dirt and grime.

Don't just clean the surfaces. Spring clean behind and around the stove every month to remove the cobwebs, both figuratively and literally!

**Stovetop Burners**

The burners symbolize the wealth-generating potential of your home. Don't neglect a broken burner even if the other three work. Be sure to repair defective burners immediately…they may just be taking an unnecessary toll on your bank account! Likewise, fix any broken knobs, switches, light fixtures and bulbs, clocks, timers—all parts of the stove should be in top-notch working condition.

Be sure to use all stovetop burners equally. It bodes well for your long-term financial prosperity.

Traditional feng shui trick: hanging a mirror over your stove's burners can double your wealth!

### *Doors*

Ideally, the kitchen should be home to only one door: the kitchen door. If there are two entrances to the kitchen, it is best that neither lies in the direct path of the stove, as the energy flowing through the doors can dampen the stove's power and vitality.

*Multiple Doors in Kitchen*

Do you have difficulty holding on to money? When multiple doors open into the kitchen, creating a direct path in front of the stove, it's important to deflect the intense energy and constant foot-traffic. Such a situation can result in interpersonal conflict and an unstable financial situation.

*Feng Shui Solution:*

- You'll need two wind chimes for this cure. Hang the wind chimes halfway between the stove and each of the doors.
- You can also slow down the energy with some potted plants.

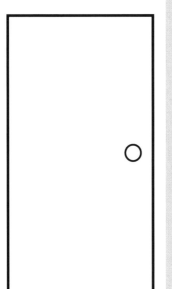

- Does one of your kitchen doors lead outside? Such a drafty setup could be adversely affecting your income. Try not to use the outside door as much.
- You can also hang a bamboo flute above the inside door frame. The flute helps to promote safety and stabilize your funds.
- If the door leads to the garage, try to offset the fumes with plants that purify the air.
- Hang a crystal ball from the center of the kitchen ceiling as an overall cure for kitchen ailments and to stimulate cash flow. Set that Intention high!

## The Bedroom

You spend about a third of every day in your bedroom, and while it doesn't influence wealth as much as your kitchen does, there are still some cash-cultivating tricks you can try. First, you must find the wealth corner of your bedroom, which takes us on a little journey through the Ba-Gua Map.

### The Ba-Gua Map

The Ba-Gua, or Feng Shui Octagon, is a simple mapping tool used by modern feng shui schools to figure out which parts of your home correspond to particular life areas. It is shaped like an octagon, with each of its eight sides relating to one of nine life sectors: Fame, Relationships, Children, Helpful People, Career, Knowledge, Family and Wealth. What's the ninth life-area? Health…and it's right in the middle! Take a moment to get acquainted with the Ba-Gua Map:

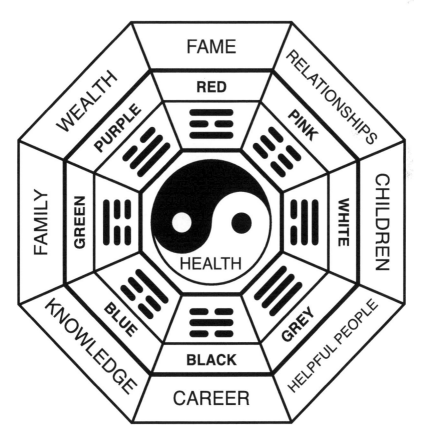

Let's start by analyzing the bedroom:

1. Stand in your bedroom's doorway, with the knowledge/career/
   helpful people sections of the octagon facing you.
2. Assess where you are according to the Ba-Gua. For instance, if
   the door to your bedroom sits in the middle of the wall, you're in
   the career area; if it is aligned to the left, you're in the knowledge
   area; if your bedroom door veers to the right, you're in the helpful
   people area.

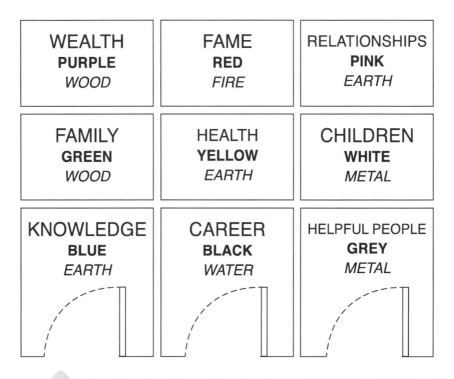

| WEALTH<br>**PURPLE**<br>*WOOD* | FAME<br>**RED**<br>*FIRE* | RELATIONSHIPS<br>**PINK**<br>*EARTH* |
|---|---|---|
| FAMILY<br>**GREEN**<br>*WOOD* | HEALTH<br>**YELLOW**<br>*EARTH* | CHILDREN<br>**WHITE**<br>*METAL* |
| KNOWLEDGE<br>**BLUE**<br>*EARTH* | CAREER<br>**BLACK**<br>*WATER* | HELPFUL PEOPLE<br>**GREY**<br>*METAL* |

You will always be in one of these three areas, whether you are
applying the Ba-Gua to a specific room or referencing your entire
home.

3. Once you've gotten your bearings, locate the other areas of the

room. As you can see, your wealth area sits in the far left corner of your bedroom.

---

*Feng Shui Solution:*

* The wealth area is linked to the element Wood. Supercharge your wealth section by hanging a wind chime in that corner.
* If your color scheme allows for it, jazz up your space with purples, greens, reds and blues, all colors associated with the wealth area.

---

Caution: Don't use water or plant elements in the wealth corner of your bedroom!

*Doors in Bedrooms*

Doors that lead outside, particularly windowed French doors that open out to a balcony or patio, sound romantic, but, according to feng shui, are problematic, both for your relationships and your finances. They can represent divorce and finances lost.

---

*Feng Shui Solution:*

* Use the doors less often.
* Place a brass wind chime in front of the door to stabilize relationships and finances.
* Hang drapes to cover the doors, especially at night when you are sleeping.

### Bedroom Tips for Overall Wealth

Your wealth is directly tied to how well you sleep. You just can't perform your best, thereby increasing wealth, if insomnia strikes. The following suggestions will help you catch more restful zzzs:

- Do not keep computers or work-related furniture and objects in your bedroom. If your bedroom doubles as a workspace, see the cures on page 33.
- Keep your nightstand free of too many books. A single novel will do.
- Mirrors, especially when placed directly in front of the bed, can keep you awake at night. Remove mirrors in inopportune places in your bedroom. See cures on page 31.
- Does your bed double as storage? Clear out everything from under your bed—clothes, shoes, books—they may be keeping you from a good night's sleep!

## Infuse Your Wealth Area with Life

Now that we've been introduced to the Ba-Gua Map, let's use it to identify the wealth area of your home.

1. Stand at your front door with the knowledge/career/helpful people sections of the octagon facing you.
2. Assess where you are according to the Ba-Gua, either in the knowledge, career or helpful people areas.
3. Once you've gotten your bearings, locate the wealth corner of your home, which will be in the far left corner.

Let's explore some feng shui tips and tricks for activating the wealth corner of your home.

## *Plant Some Prosperity*

Add some life to your wealth corner by purchasing a healthy new plant. Pay attention to lighting conditions. If your wealth corner receives an abundance of sunrays, decorate with a full sun plant. If your wealth corner is shady, purchase a shade-tolerant plant. Artificial plants work too!

> What doesn't work are dried flowers or dead branches, symbols of stagnant chi. Potpourri may smell pleasant, but it can inflict disastrous outcomes on your finances.

Green is the color of money, so opt for a green plant with coin-shaped leaves, such as jade plants (Crassula ovata) that bloom flowers of white. Succulents such as these don't need to be watered that often, and they can blossom up to twice a year. Flowers, especially reds and purples, particularly energize wealth and success.

Consider pots colored purple, red, green or gold to enliven your wealth sector even more. If your financial condition has been a bit "rocky," fill the pot with stones in order to stabilize your finances.

## *Chime in Some Cash*

Strategically place a wind chime in your wealth corner to call in some cash. Bamboo or wooden wind chimes made with four hollow rods work well for lifting chi in the wealth area. Wind chimes decorated with water-related themes, such as fish or dolphins, are also recommended.

## Water for Wealth

Free-flowing water is perhaps the most effective element with which to draw more wealth into your life. Placing a fish tank in your wealth area is just one idea. Make sure your fish are healthy and strong, and keep the fish tank clean at all times. If keeping fish is too much of a commitment for your lifestyle, invest in a flowing fountain.

Traditional feng shui recommends housing nine gold fish per tank.

You can also hang some artwork in your wealth corner. Decorate with paintings or photographs of running rivers and streams. Avoid violent depictions of stormy waters (which indicate turbulent finances) and artwork that showcases stagnant pools of water. You want that wealth constantly flowing into your life.

## Money-making Objects

Everyone has his or her own idea of wealth. Decorate the wealth corner of your home with symbols of richness that speak to you. Perhaps it's a beautiful antique jewelry box, or a citrine crystal known to stimulate abundance and prosperity.

Decorate with artwork of possessions that represent the type of wealth you desire—cars, beachfront properties, yachts…whatever speaks to you personally. You can even place your dream board in your wealth corner.

Every wealth corner deserves a round bowl or vase to place money in on a daily basis. As you drop in some coins, visualize the money multiplying. A vase of purple, gold, green or red carries enhanced activating powers.

Put an object that symbolizes wealth in front of a mirror. Voila! Your wealth may double!

### Colors to Cash in On

Notice a pattern yet? There's a reason we keep mentioning the royal colors (purple and red) and the money colors (green and gold). Feng shui history links purple to money because it was the hardest color to make. Only royalty wore purple garbs, giving the color a special connection to wealth. Green is the color of money, so that relationship speaks for itself. And who can forget the tale of Midas, the wealthy king whose touch turned everything, even his own daughter, to gold? Consider decorating with purple curtains, or placing a gold statue in your wealth corner. If red says wealth to you more than purple or gold, then by all means, place a silk red flower in a sleek modern vase to cash in on some color magic.

### Clutter-free Wealth

Feng shui teaches clutter free in all aspects of your life, including the wealth section of your home. Keep your wealth area tidy and clean in order to energize chi.

For instance, if your desk sits in the wealth sector of your house, keep it free of clutter. What is money, if not stacks of paper? And how can you invite more money into your life, if it is already jam packed with stacks upon stacks of paper?

Welcome new objects into your wealth area as you would a respected guest. Acknowledge their purpose—to bring more wealth into your life—and thank them for a job you know will be well done.

### Air-conditioners and Vents

An air-conditioner or vent in the wealth area of your home may just be blowing your money away.

> *Feng Shui Solution:*
>
> - Cut a piece of decorative fabric into long rectangular strips. Hang the cloth over the unit so that when the air blows, the strips flow through the air, symbolizing money flowing into your life. Use red or purple ribbons to represent money.
> - Always keep vents and air conditioners free of dust and grime.

## The Bathroom

Is your bathroom in your wealth area? Oh, what a drain! But don't worry; it's not the end of the world and doesn't have to drain your finances.

*Feng Shui Solution:*

- Keep your bathroom door closed at all times so that your home's energy doesn't flow into the bathroom and down the drain.
- Hang a wind chime on the outside of the bathroom door.
- Hang a mirror on the outside of the bathroom door to reflect bad chi away.
- Stop up your bathtub and sink drains, and be sure to keep your toilet lid down when not in use.
- Decorate your bathroom in greens, reds, purples and golds to attract more wealth into your life.
- Fix any plumbing issues, dripping faucets or dirty fixtures.
- It's best if your toilet is in an alcove, but if it's not, place some fresh flowers above the toilet.
- Decorate with a vase filled with eight stalks of bamboo to counteract the draining energy of the bathroom with the uplifting energy of the wood element.
- Add a bowl of crystals to your bathroom décor. Try a mix of amethyst, hematite, citrine and rose quartz.
- Mirrors should not reflect the toilet. Remove the mirror and decorate with a painting that inspires a feeling of wealth instead.
- Avoid decorating with wind chimes and candles inside the bathroom.
- Open the blinds and window during the day to stimulate active chi.
- Surround yourself with luxurious items, such as towels and soaps. If you're going to splurge, then the wealth area is the place to do it!

# The Office

Wealth is intrinsically tied to success and career, so it goes without saying that your office (including your home office) has an effect on your prosperity.

### *The Desk*

We all have a natural preference for where we like to position our desks. Some people face their desks toward a window, while others attempt to minimize distraction by facing their desks toward the wall. According to feng shui, your desk is best placed in the commanding position.

The commanding position puts you in charge…of your life, your career, your wealth! Place your desk as far away from the door as possible. Resist facing the window or the walls, and instead open your desk out to face the door. With your desk in this position you should be able to see the majority of the room from your chair. You'll have an unobstructed view of the office door so that you can see who is approaching.

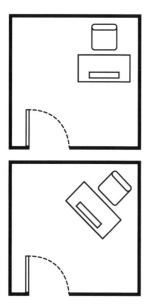

Even if you work alone at home and never receive visitors, seeing who or what is headed your way is symbolically important. Be sure not to back your desk too close to the wall. Give yourself at least four feet of space behind you. Likewise, don't barricade yourself in the corner—you should be able to access your desk from either side.

Got a glass desk? Money-making deals may just be falling through the cracks. If glass rests on top of wood, you're in business, but if you have a glass-top desk, consider trading it in for a rectangular, wood desk. Otherwise, slow down the chi by decorating your desk with some wooden accessories, like a cleverly carved pen and pencil holder, and a plant.

### The Wealth Corner

Every time the phone rings, money may be headed your way, especially if you place your phone in the wealth corner of your desk. Yes, even your desk can be separated into the nine life areas!

> *Feng Shui Solution:*
>
> ◆ Place a purple object—some purple stationary or perhaps a purple money vase—in the wealth corner of your desk to help generate more funds.

### The Wealth Area of Your Office

Supercharge the wealth corner of your office by adding some symbols of wealth. (See pages 65-67.) Here are a few ideas to refresh your memory:

* A jade plant in a red, purple, gold or green pot.
* Images, photos or pictures of your idea of wealth.
* A fountain or fish tank.
* A heavy crystal weight on your checks.
* Circles in the wealth area of your home or office are delightfully auspicious.

## The Dining Room

A well-fed soul is a wealthy soul. Use your dining room table to reflect and draw in more wealth by placing a large decorative bowl full of fruit in its center. Add a full-sized mirror on the wall across from the table to multiply the fruit and your wealth!

Oranges in particular are thought to increase wealth.

Create a feeling of wealth in your dining room with carefully chosen décor.

When decorating with plants, make sure they are healthy. Plants with nice, soft, rounded leaves are ideal.

A good quality silk plant is an option if your dining room does not provide enough light. Avoid dried flowers—they're dead energy!

Keep your dining room table clear of clutter. No homework, projects or bills on the table. Clutter represents the inability to move forward and blocks abundance from entering your life. Create space for wealth to flow!

*Feng Shui Solution:*

♦ Being in direct view of the stove while eating at the dining room table can negatively impact your back account. Place two bamboo flutes over the kitchen door at 45-degree angles. (See cure on page 41.)

## The Living Room

When it comes to your living room, the most effective way to give a boost to your wealth is to balance the elements: Fire, Metal, Earth, Water and Wood.

**Fire** represents passion and progress. An easy way to incorporate Fire into your living room is with a fireplace. Even easier? Decorate with some red pillows or throw blankets. A little bit of red can awaken some passion in your life and your finances.

**Metal** equals strength. You probably already have elements of Metal in your living room. Your computer, television and other electronics are all you need to add strength to the elemental mix.

**Earth** represents balance and helps to ground your energy so that wealth can find you. Add some stone elements to your living room, such as a stone coffee table or sculpture. Earth tones, such as brown and tan rugs, also add an element of Earth to the space.

**Water** represents flow and expansion. We've already discussed Water's ability to draw wealth into your world, so be sure to have water elements at play in your living room. A glass vase or statue ushers in the water element, as do blues and blacks.

**Wood** represents growth. Grow your bank account by adding plants and wood furniture to your living room. The color green also works.

### Windows

Windows are directly linked to wealth. If your windows are cloudy, energy is blocked. Metaphorically, you are unable to see opportunities clearly, and how can you act on opportunities for wealth if you cannot see them?

*Feng Shui Solution:*

- Keep your windows clean and your view unobstructed!

Feng Shui Tidbit: A skylight (in any room) can impact your finances, and not in a positive direction. For cures see page 47.

# Letting Wealth Enter

We've worked on increasing the flow of wealth inside your home; now, let's work on increasing the flow of wealth into your home.

*Cluttered Front Entryway*

Who wants to come home to a front entrance that's cluttered with trash, toys, dead plants, shoes, bikes, newspapers, etc.? And who (including wealth) is going to come knocking on that door? Few, is who. Keep the front entrance to your home clutter free and swept of dead leaves and dirt.

*Feng Shui Solution:*

◆ Is your entryway dark and foreboding? Brighten up that entrance so that wealth comes knocking by adding a bright light (the brighter the bulb the better). Your whole home will be energetically uplifted. Or use a bug light to keep pesky insects away.

◆ Add some plants to your entryway. Succulents are a wonderful option for expanding dark, stifling front entrances.

### Front Door

Your front door influences all the energies that enter—your health, your wealth, your career…you name it! If you are looking to increase wealth, paint your front door a money color, such as black or green.

### Fountains

Water equals wealth, remember? You can infuse your life with prosperity by adding an exterior fountain that flows towards your front door. The most effective type of fountain is one that circulates from a pool of water, rather than one that disappears in a trickle between some rocks.

Water flowing away from the door symbolizes money flowing away from your wallet!

### Hallways

Ideally, your hallways are open and clear for energy to flow. When there are too many doors in a hallway, fighting can erupt, symbolically depleting your financial reserves.

*Feng Shui Solution:*

- To soothe the frenetic energy of multiple doors, hang a crystal or wind chime from the hallway's center or from each archway. If you have a long hallway made up of doors on each side, position three wind chimes or crystals at regularly spaced intervals.
- You can also slow down the chi with some houseplants.

### Interior Stairway

If the stairway inside your house faces your front door, money may be rolling out at a far faster rate than it is rolling in. This isn't so much of an issue if the distance between the stairs and the door is greater than twice the height of the tallest family member.

*Feng Shui Solution:*

- Slow down the chi with a strategically placed plant or vase of flowers.
- Display art and photos in visually dynamic frames, and choose colors and elements that are aligned with the Ba-gua area of your staircase and front door.

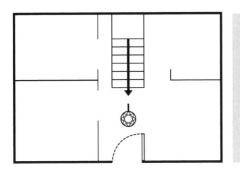

- Hang a wind chime or crystal halfway between your front door and the bottom of the stairs.

*An Uninviting Mailbox*

Even if your checks come via direct deposit, your mailbox still exerts a symbolic influence on your finances. If your mailbox is worn out or hidden from view, wealth cannot find you. Add a fresh coat of paint in a money-making color. After giving your mailbox a facelift and beautifying it a bit, see about moving it to a more visible location.

*Feng Shui Solution:*

- If you live in an apartment and cannot move your mailbox, try to invite more notice by placing your house or apartment numbers in a more visible spot. Consider adding your house numbers in multiple locations, and slant them up at a 45-degree angle to signify an increased flow of money.

*Missing Limbs*

When your home, or your home's lot, is missing limbs, so to speak, it can negatively influence every aspect of your life, including your wealth. If your house is rectangular or square in shape, you're in luck. But if your home is U-shaped or L-shaped, you're missing a corner in a life area…and that area might just be wealth. Use the Ba-Gua Map to assess which life area is missing from your home.

*Feng Shui Solution:*

- Place a mirror on the wall in the missing area to energetically fill in the gap.
- If you're more partial to plants, place some in the corner next to the missing section of your home.
- Alternately, hang or place a crystal to expand and strengthen the energy of the missing area.
- A very simple cure is to write, "This is to complete the missing wealth area of my property" on a piece of paper, stick it in a red envelope and put it behind a photo on an adjacent wall. Remember the strength of Intention!

If your lot is likewise missing life areas, plant some trees or bushes in those missing areas to cure the problem.

Feng Shui Tidbit: A hill behind your home is the ideal feng shui scenario. The land sloping upward represents the ability to hold on to your wealth.

## Traditional Feng Shui Cures for Wealth

Traditional feng shui cures are not that expensive, and if you believe in their effectiveness and set them with the right Intention, results will very likely follow.

### Feng Shui Money Tree

We've seen the Feng Shui Money Tree crop up in many of the suggested solutions. There are three different types of feng shui money trees:

- Jade Tree (Crassula ovata)
- Guiana Chestnut or Saba Nut, also commonly referred to as a Money Tree (Pachira aquatica)
- Chinese Coins Money Tree—an artificial tree with Chinese coins hanging from the limbs

### Lucky Bamboo

There's nothing quite like a lucky bamboo plant to draw happiness, health and abundance into your home. An indoor bamboo plant should incorporate each of the five elements:

**Wood** – the bamboo
**Earth** – rocks to fill the pot
**Water** – an inch of water to help the bamboo grow
**Fire** – tie a red ribbon or put the bamboo in a red pot
**Metal** – house the bamboo plant in a glass or metal pot

Lucky bamboo is from a species called Dracaena sanderiana and can be mildly toxic, so keep out of reach of children and pets.

### Feng Shui Coins

Feng shui coins are considered lucky charms when it comes to bringing more wealth into your world. You can place Chinese coins in your wealth corner, on your desk, or in a clean drawer (the coins don't have to be visible for the cure to work). You can also carry feng shui coins in your pocket or purse, or wear them as a necklace or pendant.

Chinese coins are also arranged on a red and gold tassel. Three Chinese golden coins tied together in a mystic knot of red symbolizes the trinity of luck from heaven, earth and mankind. The mystic knot is said to strengthen and enhance the money cure.

### Jade Buddha

A Feng Shui Jade Buddha is a symbol of prosperity and can help attract wealth. Jade is a healing gem that wards off bad energy and balances and harmonizes chi. If a Buddha statue doesn't appeal to you, consider applying a cure in the form of a different jade statue that speaks to your tastes. You can even wear jade jewelry for the same effect, as long as you power it with the Intention to increase your finances.

### Dragon Head Turtle

You might not think the Dragon Head Turtle is the most attractive (the head of a dragon with a coin in its mouth and the body of a tortoise) but it represents good luck, longevity, protection, harmony and money in feng shui, particularly a new and prosperous business venture.

### Fu Dogs

Feng Shui Fu Dogs are a traditional symbol of wealth and status that were placed in front of wealthy homes, Imperial palaces, temples and government offices. If Fu Dogs symbolize wealth to you, then it may just be an effective cure. Remember, it's setting an Intention and belief to the cures.

### Money Frog

Also known as the Jin Chan, the three-legged money frog brings good news as it relates to prosperity. This ancient feng shui relic is said to stimulate the flow of money into the home. Do not position your money frog facing the door, as you don't want funds spilling out of the home. A money frog should never be placed in the bathroom, bedroom, dining room or kitchen.

Feng shui is an ancient art. Tradition is meant to be transformed. You can add your own flare and style to any of the aforementioned wealth cures. If a three-legged money frog doesn't work with your décor, then why not use a sculpture that appeals to you on an aesthetic level and represents money? A bouquet of flowers made out of dyed bills perhaps? Don't be afraid to put your own personal stamp on these cures.

Everyone's idea of wealth is different, as is everyone's way of obtaining abundance.

❖ *Chapter Three* ❖

# YOUR CAREER

Each person's measure of career success is different. To some, career success is linked to the size of their bank account. To others, it's wrapped up in their reputation or degree of fame. Some associate career success with travel opportunities. Others, with the number and quality of connections they've secured. Still others equate career success with the knowledge and wisdom they've garnered. *Feng Shui on a Dime* has all these life areas covered to make sure your career is in first-rate order.

First stop? Your office, where career success begins.

## The Office

**Let's take a look at the ideal office scenario. Check the boxes that apply.**

❑   Your office is located toward the back of the building.

> The rear of the building holds the most power. That's not to say you want to work out of a dark, dingy office in the back over a bright, spacious one in the front, but ideally you have the best of both worlds. Likewise, an office on an upper floor is best placed as far from the elevators as possible.

❑   Your office has a regular shape (rectangular or square).

❑   Your office gets natural light and has at least one window.

❑   Your office has a solid door.

❑   Your desk is as far from the door as possible and does not lie in the direct path of the door.

❑   You have a clear view of the door from your seated position at your desk.

❑   Your desk is rectangular and made of wood.

Curved and rounded desks are also auspicious.

❑   You can access your desk from either side.

❑   Your desk doesn't sit too close to the wall or directly in front of a window.

❑   Your chair is sturdy, with no gap between the seat and the back, and reaches to at least the top of your shoulders.

There's only so much control you have over your office (unless you work from home). But don't worry! We're here to troubleshoot potential challenges.

Let's take a look at some common office predicaments.

*Inauspiciously Placed Office*

Most of the time we don't get to choose where our offices are located, unless, of course, we're the boss. There's a simple feng shui cure to energetically pull your office to the back of the building and ramp up your power.

*Feng Shui Solution:*

+ Hang a large mirror on the office wall that is nearest the back of the building. The mirror should be facing your desk. The mirror doesn't have to be visible; you can hide it behind a piece of artwork if that's more business appropriate.

*Misshapen Office*

A square or rectangular-shaped office may not be all that architecturally interesting, but it bodes well for your career. If your office is irregularly shaped or missing life areas, try the following enhancement cures.

*Feng Shui Solution:*

+ Hang a mirror along the walls of the missing area. In this way you are drawing energy to it and "completing the square."
+ To enhance further, position a bright light at the missing corner of the area.
+ Line the walls of the missing area with an odd number of plants.

Traditional cure: If your office is a mess of irregular shapes and angles, purchase nine new plants on the same day and position the plants in an arrangement that best balances the room.

*Sharp Corners and Intruding Columns*

Projecting corners and columns can disrupt the flow of chi through your office, especially if a sharp corner points directly at you when you are seated at your desk.

*Feng Shui Solution:*

- Soften sharp corners by placing a large plant in front of the edges.
- Plants can also be hung in front of a protruding corner.
- Reposition your desk so that it is not directly in line with the protruding corner.

*Glass Walls*

Check in with your inner feng shui consultant. Glass walls are a positive because you are more approachable and better able to keep track of what's happening in the office. If the glass walls of your office make you feel jittery or distracted, then try the following cure.

*Feng Shui Solution:*

- Hang blinds to cover the glass. Even if you never draw the blinds, they offer a sense of peace and security.

*Fluorescent Lights*

Working under fluorescent lights has been linked to various negative health effects including:

- Headaches/migraines
- Eye strain
- Insomnia due to melatonin suppression
- Depression
- Endocrine disruption and ill-functioning immune system
- Female hormonal/menstrual cycle disruption
- Increases in breast cancer rates and tumor formation
- Stress/anxiety due to cortisol suppression
- Sexual development/maturation disruption
- Obesity

If you cannot change the fluorescent bulbs to a full-spectrum alternative such as grow lights, then add some softer, incandescent lighting to your workspace. The lighting from your desk lamp or floor lamp can offset harsh, fluorescent bulbs overhead.

*Cubicles*

Cubicles can drain an individual's creativity and sense of purpose. The partitions offer moderate privacy and the distractions floating around the shared space can be overwhelming. Most of the time, you don't even have a solid desk on which to work, but a countertop! The first thing to address when working from a cubicle is to set yourself up in the commanding position.

**The Commanding Position:** Placing yourself in the eye-line of the cubicle entrance may not be possible. But you can use the following adjustments to strengthen your workspace and supercharge your ability to thrive in your career.

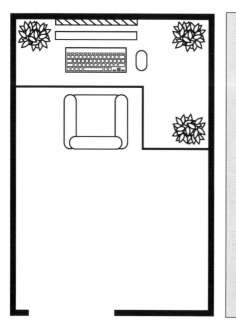

*Feng Shui Solution:*

♦ Rather than using the reflection of your computer monitor to keep track of who's behind you, hang an 8 x 10 inch mirror so that you can see the entrance. Find a frame that inspires you. Rather than having a vanity mirror, you'll have yourself a piece of art!

**Overhead Storage Bins:** Storage bins above your desk space not only make you feel cramped, but can also hamper your rise up the corporate ladder. To diffuse the negative effects, hang one crystal ball per every four feet of storage.

**Infuse Your Cubicle with Life**: The chi rushing through office cubicles can be intense and distracting. Adding life in the form of an odd number of plants or a small fountain can draw and keep balanced energy inside your cubicle. If you can't decorate with a fountain, consider adding a photo or painting of a river or waterfall to stimulate chi and increase your salary.

Whether you have a separate office or a cubicle, be sure to reclaim your individualism and activate your creativity by decorating with accessories and artwork that inspire productivity and innovation.

# Let's Talk Desk

Your desk is understandably the most important piece of furniture in your office. We discussed the importance of arranging your desk in the command position (see page 71) but the type of desk and shape of desk are also key factors in career success.

**Desk Shape:** The best shape is rectangular, with curved and round shapes also ranking high. Missing corners are problematic, as are L-shaped desks, which can compromise your view of the door. The sturdier and more secure the better, with side panels and a front panel that reach to the floor.

*Rectangle:* A rectangular desk promotes concentration and stability.

*Circle:* A circular desk enhances creativity and brainstorming.

*Curved:* A curved desk increases concentration because the energy flows towards you. The outside curve keeps people from overstaying their welcome.

*Front Panel:* A desk with a closed front (a panel that reaches to the floor) helps to establish boundaries.

*Open Front:* A desk with an open front encourages intimacy and interaction with coworkers and clients.

**Desk Type:** Dining room tables aren't desks. Neither is a piece of plywood or a door propped up onto two filing cabinets. A sturdy desk (that was designed to be used only as a desk) is the best option for fortifying career success.

Most feng shui experts agree that wood desks are your best bet, but every element has advantages.

*Wood:* Solid, reliable, supportive, long lasting

*Metal:* Sharp, promotes mental energy and concentration

*Glass:* Revealing and intimate

Glass desks must be balanced with wood objects and plants, as the glass lets money and deals slip away. (The exception is a glass tabletop that rests on a solid wood desk.)

**Desk Size:** While a large desk symbolizes productivity and authority, a desk that is disproportionately large to its space can promote lose of control and command. It is important to keep the size of your desk proportional to your office space.

**Desk Color:** The color of your desk is a matter of preference and consideration of the type of work you do. Wooden desks or neutral-colored surfaces help to alleviate visual strain because they contrast well with white paper.

*Black:* Encourages the flow of energy inward, which activates inner awareness and stimulates opportunities.

*White:* Enlivens chi and mental faculties, but can drain the physical body. Avoid if your health is compromised.

*Brown:* Strengthens the physical body.

*Gray:* Laser beams the mind but can have an adverse effect on physical energy.

*Green:* Balances both body and mind, and strengthens stamina.

*Neutral:* Stimulates mental energy without draining the body. A good alternative to gray and white.

*Bright Tones:* Visually stimulating but can distract the body and mind.

One last note about the desk: Messy cords and clutter at your feet can constrict and impede career growth. Do not keep a trashcan or a chaotic tangle of cords under your desk. You can hide cords behind a wall, or with a cable wall hiding system.

### *Map Your Desk*

Apply the Ba-Gua Map to your desk to stimulate certain aspects of your career.

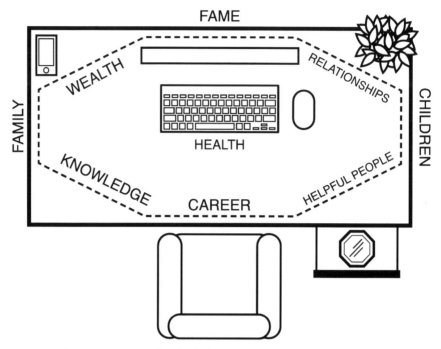

Start at the entrance to the desk (the career area), which is where you sit at the center of the desk. Locate the other life areas around you.

**Wealth:** To stimulate income, place your phone in the wealth corner of your desk. You can activate your money-earning potential by adding some purple stationary to your wealth sector. The wealth sector of your desk is also a great place for a healthy plant or a vase of blooming flowers.

**Fame:** To enhance your reputation, put a bright lamp in the fame area of your desk. Attach red fabric underneath the fame area for an even stronger reputation. The fame area is also a great place for a nameplate, business cards...any memento that highlights your accomplishments.

**Family:** To encourage cooperation among coworkers and clients, place a healthy plant in the family area of your desk. Got family photos? Frame them in wood and let them perch in the family corner of your desk.

**Children:** To increase communication, put a brass bell or singing bowl in the children corner of your desk. To stimulate creativity, add a metal object, a journal if you're a writer, a sketchbook if you're an artist...you get the picture!

**Career:** Secure a piece of black fabric under the career section of your desk as an overall enhancement. Add your favorite motivational quote here. Change it up weekly!

**Helpful People and Knowledge:** Place an octagon-shaped mirror (shiny side up) in the drawers beneath the helpful people and knowledge areas. If you're looking for travel opportunities, place a photo of your dream destination here.

Position your computer in any life area you'd like to enhance. In the knowledge area, it promotes wisdom, in the wealth area it stimulates profits, in the fame area it strengthens your reputation. Avoid positioning your computer in the family area.

## Map Your Office

Of course you can, and should, use the Ba-Gua to map your entire office. Once you've identified each of the life areas, you can apply specific cures. For instance, if you are looking to grow wiser, add some red, a bookshelf or a globe to the knowledge area.

## The Elements

Placing each of the five elements in their corresponding life areas can have a dramatic impact on career success.

### Wood

Wood belongs in the family area, where it activates your career with upward movement and expansion. Add the following feng shui solutions to the family area of your office:

*Feng Shui Solution:*

- A healthy green plant.
- Green or blue artwork.
- A rectangular object, such as a file cabinet.

### Fire

Add the fire element to the fame corner to create more movement in your career and to help you become better known and more well respected. Apply the following cures:

*Feng Shui Solution:*

- A candle or bright light.
- Anything red.
- A triangular or pyramid-shaped object that points upward.

## Earth

The earth element belongs in the center of your office, right smack dab in the health space. Experiment with some more earth and you'll feel calmer, more balanced and connected to other people and opportunities. Add the following earth cures to your environment:

*Feng Shui Solution:*

- A ceramic or stone pot or sculpture.
- Artwork in yellow and earth tones.
- Any square or cube-shaped furniture, such as stereo speakers.
- An area rug in earth tones.

## Metal

When added to the children area of your office, Metal strengthens communication and unlocks creativity. Enhance your career with the following metal cures:

*Feng Shui Solution:*

- Anything metal: a chair, table, artwork, etc.
- Any pictures containing white.
- A circular object.

## Water

Water in the career sector of your office will improve clarity and wisdom, increase earning potential and bring the right contacts into your sphere. Water can be added in any of the following ways:

*Feng Shui Solution:*

◆ Decorate with black and dark blue.
◆ Artwork that depicts water images.
◆ Add a fountain.
◆ Any object with a wavy, spiral shape.

Images of still water help to stimulate wisdom and clarity.

## The Bedroom

The bedroom is the lover's domain, which we will discuss in depth in Chapter 4, but there are a few adjustments you can make to the bedroom to strengthen career success.

### A Sturdy Headboard

A solid headboard with no gaps, holes or bars can promote career advancement. If you can shake the headboard, then it's not sturdy enough!

Never place an object—such as a chaise lounge or chest—that extends above the foot of your bed. It can block career and travel opportunities.

*Toilet Above or Next to Bedroom*

If your bedroom is directly below or shares a common wall with a toilet, career success could be blocked.

*Feng Shui Solution:*

- If your bed is directly underneath or adjacent to the toilet, move your bed to an alternate position in the bedroom.
- Decorate the bathroom with light colors so the energy is lifted and doesn't sink into the bedroom.
- Mirrors, in general, don't belong in the bedroom, but a mirror hidden behind the headboard (reflective side facing the bed) will deflect the energy from the toilet. The mirror should be as wide as the bed and reach lengthwise to the top of the head-board.

Crown moldings on the walls and ceiling help, because they provide an additional barrier between the bathroom and bedroom.

*Cluttered Entryway*

The entrance to your bedroom should be free of clutter. If the entryway is too narrow it can harm your career prospects. Implement the following cure.

*Feng Shui Solution:*

- Hang a mirror on each side of the entryway.

Hang a wind chime over any narrow entrance in order to expand both the entryway and your opportunities!

*Exterior Door in Bedroom*

If the chi flows directly from your bedroom door, across the foot of your bed, to an outside door in the bedroom, career opportunities may be rushing past and out the door. Your health may also be impacted.

*Feng Shui Solution:*

+ Hang a faceted crystal in the center of the room to diffuse the energy.

## Bedroom Career Cures

- Tie three coins together with red ribbon and place on your nightstand to invite a steady stream of income into your life. You can also purchase a ready made feng shui 3-coin charm.
- If you're the kind of person who likes keepsakes and wish chests, then you'll probably enjoy creating a wealth vase. You can fill your wealth vase with crystals, diamonds, jewelry...whatever connects you to financial success in your career. Keep your wealth vase hidden inside an armoire, closet or cabinet in your bedroom. Make sure the wealth vase doesn't face the door, as you want the wealth streaming in, not out.
- Turtles and three-legged frogs are traditionally seen as auspicious. A turtle or frog statue in the career corner of your bedroom can help promote career success. Personalize with a career statue of meaning to you!
- Recharge career success with a bright light on your dressing table. Himalayan salt lamps are natural, energy-enhancing alternatives.
- Make sure your bedroom door is solid and sturdy.

*Strengthen Your Inner Wisdom*

The bedroom offers an ideal enhancement for the knowledge area of your life, which is directly linked to your career. Hang a crystal ball over the head of your bed.

You can also hang a crystal or place a decorative crystal in the knowledge area of your home (front left).

## The Career Area

The career area is located at your home's front entrance. Sprinkling some cures in this sector will help you secure that promotion, earn more money and strengthen your reputation.

Stay away from objects made of earth materials. They "muddy" your career. Try not to decorate with square or flat objects in the career area of your home.

*Water*

We've already discussed how Water in the career sector of your office activates success and abundance. Adding the water element to your front entrance has the same effect.

Never place a fountain in a fame area of your home, as it can "dampen" your reputation.

*Feng Shui Solution:*

- Add in the moving water element with a fountain that flows into the home. A circular fountain in front of your home bodes well for career and financial success, but make sure the water does not get stagnant or dirty.
- Add an aquarium filled with multi-colored, active fish, which boost your ability to work well with many different types of people.
- Place a vase of fresh flowers and water at your home's entrance.
- Add in the moving water element figuratively with a picture of a calmly running river. (Paintings of crashing waves are too chaotic and can negatively influence your career trajectory.)
- Paintings of a still lake or pond help to cultivate wisdom. Metal supports Water, so consider framing images in silver, metal frames.
- Light your interior with a lamp with a metal or glass base. Blue, black or dark-gray lampshades are the most auspicious.
- Decorate with wave-shaped, undulating objects.

Metal, glass and crystal objects also invite a water element into your career area.

### Colors

The career area of your home or business is best accented in black. Avoid decorating with earth tones such as yellow.

Add in a crystal bowl full of colorful crystals. Lapis lazuli, smoky quartz, hematite, citrine and jet exhibit powerful influences on career growth.

### *The Front Door*

Consider painting your front door black or red to draw in wealth and opportunity.

Traditional cure: firecrackers hung over the front door (inside the house) can help stimulate new revenue sources.

Support a balanced flow of energy into your home by using the front door as much as possible. Back doors are for special deliveries, not for millionaires and heads of companies! Every time you open the door a dose of chi flows through your home, ushering in better health, wealth and career success.

Make sure your front door is in working order—hinges, doorknobs and doorbells all fully functional. A door that swings open and closed on its own can block money and helpful people from entering your life.

### *The Front Entrance*

We've already discussed the importance of an inviting front entrance. Light your porch so that it can be easily seen from the street in order to invite chi into your space. Make sure your front path is swept clean and free of clutter so that your career path likewise remains unobstructed.

### *Plants*

Evergreen shrubs accelerate career growth and Narcissus plants are good luck when you are looking for a job. Avoid warming your front entrance with plants that have thorns, including rose bushes and cacti, as they can have a deleterious impact on your career.

### Fireplaces

Water is the dominant element of your career sector, and a fire in your home's career area may dampen your prospects.

*Feng Shui Solution:*

- Position one plant in front of the mouth of the fireplace.
- For a more advanced cure, place nine plants around the fireplace and on the mantel.
- Hang a mirror over the mantel of the fireplace to balance the fire element with the water element.

## Home's Position

Your neighborhood and the position of your home relative to the street can have a huge impact on the flow of positive energy into your life. The ideal neighborhood is rich in lush, vibrant foliage, healthy, energetic animals and friendly people.

Your street funnels chi into your life. A street with rushing traffic bombards you with frenetic energy that can destabilize many life areas, particularly your career, helpful people and knowledge sectors. Essentially, a busy street can—quite literally—suck the chi right out of you. In a similar fashion, a street that is too sleepy doesn't provide enough chi, and your life areas can become "starved" for energy. Like most things in life, you're looking for a happy medium.

Three scenarios in particular can have undesirable impacts on your opportunities for career growth.

## Cul-de-sac

We discussed the influence living at the end of a cul-de-sac can have on your health. Such an arrangement can also block career opportunities and make it difficult to move forward with your life. For a detailed look at suggested cures—such as adding a water element to your lot or hanging a bird feeder on your front porch—see page 44. Here are some additional recommendations.

Adding a fountain also helps with networking and strengthening connections!

*Feng Shui Solution:*

♦ Add some movement to your garden, such as a solar-powered garden sculpture.

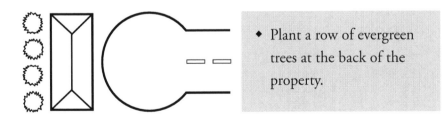

♦ Plant a row of evergreen trees at the back of the property.

## Dead-end

If your house sits at the dead end of a street you might find that you have limited career opportunities. You can invite more energy into your home by trimming back overgrowth and keeping your lawn well maintained. Make sure all your light fixtures are working, and de-clutter that lawn. Don't leave tricycles, toys or garden and land-scaping tools outside.

*One-way Street*

A one-way street has the opposite effect of a cul-de-sac. Often, there is too much energy rushing by your house. To balance this rush of energy try one of the following solutions.

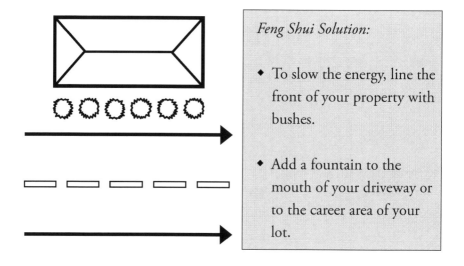

*Feng Shui Solution:*

♦ To slow the energy, line the front of your property with bushes.

♦ Add a fountain to the mouth of your driveway or to the career area of your lot.

## The Living Room

Ideally, your living room is the first room you see when you walk through your front door. Decorate with different colors to help stimulate your interaction with others who can help advance your career. If your career has been chaotic, center your life by decorating with earth tones such as yellow, brown and gold. If you are looking to add some growth and fun, decorate with blues and greens. Avoid aggressive colors in the living room, such as red. Accents of black also help to enhance career.

> *Feng Shui Solution:*
>
> ◆ Position your television or stereo in the knowledge or helpful
>   people areas of your home or living room to help increase clari-
>   ty and career opportunities.

Keep windows and blinds open so that healthy chi can circulate
through and around the home.

## The Knowledge Area

We've sprinkled suggestions for activating your knowledge area
throughout this chapter, but let's bullet point some effective enhancements. These solutions can be applied to the knowledge area of your
home, or to the knowledge areas of specific rooms in your home.

*Feng Shui Solution:*

+ Enhance your knowledge by adding the colors black, blue and green.
+ Add an animal charm to increase wisdom and help stimulate career advancement. Turtles, elephants and snakes are associated with wisdom and self-improvement.
+ The knowledge area is linked to the earth element. Adding a globe, especially a crystal globe, can give your career an extraordinary boost.
+ Play up the earth element by adding ceramic or porcelain vases or sculptures.
+ Add a painting of a mountain with a waterfall to promote knowledge and creativity.

Happen to have a brick wall or mosaic tiles in the knowledge area of your home? You're in luck! That's a symbol of the earth element.

### Crystals

Hang crystals or prisms in your knowledge corner so that they can reflect the sunlight and increase your clarity.

Note: Crystals are alive. As such, they absorb negative energy. If this negative energy isn't released every so often, it could adversely affect you and your family. To release negative energy from your crystals, expose your crystals to the energizing rays of the sun and moon (especially a full moon) for 24 hours. You can also smudge your crystals with white sage by holding the gem within the smoke for approximately four minutes.

# Helpful People/Travel Area

The helpful people and travel corner go hand in hand. Learn to harness the power of the people around you and encourage travel (both business and vacation) in your life by implementing the following enhancements.

*Feng Shui Solution:*

- Add accents of white, gray, silver and black to your helpful people area (front right).
- Add a metal or water element, such as a metal fountain.
- Place objects or symbols of guardian angels in your helpful people area. It may be a photo of a loved one or a religious figure or deity you pray to. Devotional altars are especially effective.
- Electronically powered objects activate energy and when placed in the helpful people area can draw lively and entertaining people your way.
- Add a photo of someone in your field whom you respect and whose career you'd like to emulate.
- Figurines and paintings of dolphins symbolize guides who can steer you in the right career and life direction.
- Add a picture of your dream vacation spot to this corner of your home to help manifest vacation opportunities. This cure also extends to business. For instance, if you'd like to secure an overseas transfer to France, then decorate with a painting of the Eifel Tower.

Do not add fountains or prayer altars to the helpful people corner of your bedroom, as such enhancements can lead to sleeplessness.

Any of the aforementioned cures can be applied to the helpful people areas of your home or to individual rooms.

Career satisfaction, like health, impacts each and every life area. Everyone has a career…from the CEO of a Fortune 500 company to the CEO of your home. Whether your life's mission is to direct a non-profit, excel in the role of stay-at-home mom or start your own company, it's important to choose a career that empowers and enlivens you. There are too few hours in the day and too few years of your life to remain in a stagnant job that drains your chi. A combination of cures from this chapter will help you rise through the ranks, and can even give you the foundation in which to transition from a lackluster job to a career that leads to your bliss. Your health, your wealth and your love are bound to follow!

# Chapter Four

# YOUR LOVE LIFE

Want to bring in your soulmate relationship? Are you anxiously awaiting that marriage proposal? Or maybe you're just looking for a bit more passion and lust in your life? Boy oh boy do we have some treats for you!

Before we doctor up your love life with some feng shui, let's address what your love life really means. When we mention your love life, we aren't just referring to romantic love. Your love life extends to the love you have for your children, your family members, your friends…even the stranger on the street corner begging for a quarter. And let's not forget self-love, because how can you truly love others if you're having a hard time loving yourself?

Why limit your love life to just one other? Adding some zing to your love life will improve your relationships across the board. The world could use a little bit more love. Are you up for the challenge?

Yes! Let's start with the room where love begins—the bedroom!

## The Bedroom

**Check the boxes that apply to your bedroom.**

❑   The bedroom is located in the back half of your home.

Ideally, your bedroom occupies your home's commanding position. If your front door is angled right, then the commanding position is at the back left of your house, and if the front door is angled left, then your bedroom is best located in the far right corner of your home.

❑ There is only one door leading into and out of the bedroom.

❑ Windows sit at a healthy distance from your bed.

❑ The bedroom is either square or rectangular in shape.

❑ Not too large and not too small, the bedroom is moderately sized.

If the bedroom is too big, fill the space by adding plants.

❑ The entryway is not too narrow and provides a clear, direct path into the bedroom.

❑ The bedroom door opens wide and is not hindered by objects hanging on the back of the door or furniture placed behind the door.

❑ The bedroom is used for sleeping and intimacy only and is free of all media (phones, televisions, stereos, computers, etc.).

See Chapter 1 (page 32) for more info on how electronics in the bedroom can affect your health.

❑   The bedroom is not a second office. There are no bookshelves, desks and stacks of bills on the nightstands.

❑   The bedroom is lightly furnished.

Tall, bulky furniture can stifle your psyche and your romantic opportunities. (See page 31.)

Don't worry if your bedroom is less than ideal in location or setup. We'll address some of the most common feng shui flubs below.

*Oddly Shaped Bedroom*

We've already discussed how a misshapen bedroom can affect your health (see page 27). An irregularly shaped room can also lead to relationship/marriage problems. An overall cure for bedroom ailments is to hang a crystal from the center of the room to balance energies. For more detailed fixes refer to Chapter 1 (page 28).

*Multiple Doors*

Many people consider French doors leading out to a balcony from the bedroom an ideal arrangement, but according to feng shui, the bedroom should have only one door—the entryway to the room. (This limitation does, of course, exclude the closet doors.)

Multiple doors in the bedroom can drain energy from your relationships, leading to loss of passion and an increase in conflict. A door that leads outside can signal the absence of lovers or the possibility of divorce. Try to avoid using the outside door, and hang a brass wind chime in front of the door to contain the energy of the bedroom and to stabilize your relationships. A bathroom door in the bedroom is perhaps one of the worst offenders when it comes to weakening the vital energy of your relationships.

*Feng Shui Solution:*

- To counteract the negative effects, hang a full-length mirror on the outside of the bathroom door.
- Keep the bathroom door closed.

It's better to have a bathroom door than an open space leading into the master bathroom. You can close this gap by adding curtains or beads across the opening to the bathroom.

*Fireplace in Bedroom*

In Chapter 1 (page 36) we discuss how a fireplace in the bedroom can quite literally burn up your energy. Likewise, a relationship under the influence of a fireplace could be suffering from tension and strain.

*Feng Shui Solution:*

- Hang a large painting of trees or water images above the fireplace mantel.

- Stop lighting fires and cover the opening with a potted plant.

*Mirrors in the Bedroom*

An age-old feng shui belief is that mirrors in the bedroom invite a third person into your relationship. Unless you're looking for a ménage à trois, keep mirrors out of the bedroom, and never position mirrors directly across from the bed. Mirrors in the bedroom should ideally be placed behind a closet door.

*Clashing Doors*

Are you and your loved ones getting on each other's nerves? When two doors clash, such as a closet door knocking against the bedroom door, arguments may ensue and communication can be hindered.

*Feng Shui Solution:*

- The simplest solution is to keep one of the doors closed while you open the other.
- Traditional feng shui advises hanging two red drapery tassels on the shared sides of each of the doorknobs.

*Restricted Entrance*

If the entryway to your bedroom is restricted—let's say the first thing you see when you walk into your bedroom is a closet wall or a piece of tall, heavy furniture—then you may have trouble inviting lasting relationships into your life. Whether the entryway to your bedroom is blocked, narrow or dark, take advantage of the following cures.

*Feng Shui Solution:*

- Add a bright light outside the entrance to your bedroom to light a dark entryway and activate romance.
- If your bedroom's entrance is narrow and constricted, hang a mirror on the outside of the door.

*Blocked Exit*

The same principles apply when you exit your bedroom. If the first thing you see when you walk out of your bedroom is a cumbersome bookshelf, bathroom door or closet, you may be experiencing a block in your love life.

*Feng Shui Solution:*

- Hang a convex mirror (a mirror that curves outward) on the closet door in front of you. The mirror should be eye level with the tallest occupant.
- If you are dealing with a bathroom door, hang a full-length mirror on the outside.
- You can also hang a wind chime equidistant between the two.

### Applying the Ba-Gua

You can map out your bedroom with the Ba-Gua to enhance different life areas. Of particular importance to your love life is the marriage area of your bedroom, which symbolizes love regardless of whether marriage is your ultimate goal.

Be careful of the following arrangement in the marriage/relationship corner (back right corner) of your bedroom.

*Angled Walls*

When an angled wall makes up the relationship area of your bedroom you might find yourself continually embroiled in arguments with loved ones.

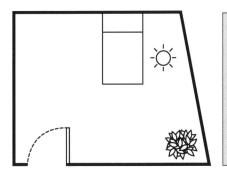

*Feng Shui Solution:*

◆ Place a light, like a Himalayan salt lamp, on one end of the angled wall and a plant on the other.

### Adding Romance to Your Marriage Corner

• Decorate this corner with symbols of romance, such as a painting of two lovers or an artistic representation of the word love.

Remove photos of family or relatives who have passed, along with any images that are dark, gloomy or threatening. Keep goth art out of the love corner!

• Decorate in twos, such as two red candles you can light each evening to ignite more passion into your life. (Electric candles are a great option!)
• Place a bowl of rose quartz crystals, or "love stones," in your marriage corner. Rose quartz crystals carry the vibration of

unconditional love and can help call in a soulmate relationship and heal any love-related issues.

You can also jazz up your love life by placing a bowl of rose quartz crystals in your bathroom, carrying the stones in your purse, placing a couple under your pillow, or wearing a rose quartz pendant. Pink tourmaline and amber also work!

- Try to incorporate red and pink, such as love-affirming quotes written in pink letters.

### Setting an Intention

Remember how Intention accounts for 70% of feng shui's effectiveness? Test it out yourself by setting a love Intention in the relationship corner of your bedroom. All it takes is a white piece of paper and a red pen (glossy pink or passionate purple inks will do the trick too).

1. Write a list of your partner's ideal qualities. Is he a social butterfly or a homebody? Does she love to travel? Is he athletic, artsy or both? Don't censor yourself or your expectations. Create your Mr. or Ms. Charming exactly as you'd like them!
2. Place the list in a decorative box along with either an image of two peonies, or two silk peonies. Assess your love life after 49 days. Hopefully you'll be enjoying a surge of romance.

Peonies represent romance, prosperity and a happy marriage.

### Adding Romance to the Relationship Corner of Every Room

Once you've added some romantic potions to the marriage area of your bedroom, you can further attract love by spicing up other relationship areas in your home. The relationship sector is located in the back right-hand corner of your home, or each individual room depending on what you are mapping. Remember, you can even activate the partnership corner of your desk! And it doesn't have to be about romance; you can set the Intention to nurture a happy, loving relationship with yourself.

The basics apply, no matter the room:

- Work with the fire element in your relationship area by adding pink, red and white for potent activating power.

Is your relationship corner in your kitchen? Then get creative with a red toaster and matching blender!

- Add photos, paintings, figurines, red or pink candles, crystals—whatever object symbolizes your ideal relationship. Electrify it with Intention!
- Add a quote or positive affirmation of love to remind you that your soulmate is headed your way.
- Add a light to the relationship corner of your home (or any room). Keep it burning bright. We recommend a Himalayan salt lamp, which also releases healthful negative ions into your home.

*A Missing Love and Relationship Area*

Your love life may be stagnant because it is missing from your home. No need to move; just implement one or more of the following cures.

*Feng Shui Solution:*

- Fill in the missing corner with a deck, boulder or pair of large red flowering plants.
- Plant a tree and hang a romantic wind chime from one of its limbs. The chime could be made of rose quartz, decorated with hearts, adorned with Cupid's bow and arrow…whatever symbolizes love to you!
- If alterations to the outside of the property aren't feasible, then hang or place a crystal in the missing corner inside. You can also add a romantic representation, such as a positive affirmation or a painting of two lovers, in the missing sector.

### Make Room for Two

If you are single and looking to be part of a duo, employ the trick of twos and arrange the room as if two people already live there. Remove any photos/artwork of just one person (from every room) to avoid a chronically single fate. Even a photo of a single bird could dash your potential for romance and lasting relationships. Decorate in even pairs. Instead of one throw pillow, decorate with two, four or six. Don't have a single reading lamp on your side of the bed. Balance out the energy and add a reading lamp on his side of the bed, even if you haven't met him yet.

Already part of a couple? Avoid decorating in threes (3 pillows, 3 candles, etc.).

The same rule of two applies to your office—use two paperweights instead of one, especially if placed at the relationship corner of your desk. Investing in an electric toothbrush? Buy a set of two, instead of just one. You get the hang of it!

### Nightstands

Nightstands say it all. If you only have one nightstand and it's on your side of the bed, then you aren't exactly calling a partner into your life.

> *Feng Shui Solution:*
>
> * Position a nightstand on each side of the bed. The nightstands should be similar (same style, weight, color, height). If you have a lamp on one nightstand, make sure you have a lamp of the same height and density on the other.

### Closets

Leave some breathing room in your closet. This not only helps chi flow more freely through your life (which benefits health), but also creates the space for a partner to move in.

Consider delegating a drawer to your future love. Set your Intention and leave the drawer empty, or fill it with some overnight toiletries for your future mate, like a toothbrush, razors and shaving cream to activate some romance in your life.

## The Bed

The bed is the centerpiece of your love life for obvious reasons that would cause us to blush were we to expand on the how and whys.

It's imperative to have your bed set up for two, which means no twin beds, and trading in that double for a queen if possible.

**Bed Size**

King-sized beds are too big and promote a divide between you and your partner. There's a physical explanation for this phenomenon. Typically, the box spring is made up of two separate pieces that literally and symbolically divide the bed in two, creating a physical chasm between you and your lover. A king-sized box spring is better, but still encourages distance between you and your mate. If you don't want to ditch your king, you can apply the cure below.

On the plus size, king-sized beds are square and represent the earth element, which can help support long-term relationships.

*Feng Shui Solution:*

• Protect the mattress (and your love life) from the split frame by adding a red, king-sized sheet between the mattress and the box springs.

Twin beds are out for obvious reasons, and even double beds are too small, but queen beds seem to be just the right fit. They're roomy without encouraging too much distance. Because they are rectangular, queen beds represent the wood element, thereby encouraging growth in your relationship.

**Bed Type**

*Wood:* Wood beds are preferable because they provide an insulating element, which makes them softer, warmer and more conducive to health, restful sleep and solid relationships.

*Metal:* Beds with metal frames, on the other hand, can exert a negative influence on your health and relationships. Metal is a powerful element, and whether it's metal from the frame or metal in the mattress and box springs, the magnetic field can wreak havoc on many different aspects of your life. In addition, metal doesn't channel energy as effectively as other feng shui elements do, such as wood.

*Water:* Waterbeds are a rarity these days, as the majority of people have caught on to the fact that while comfortable, waterbeds aren't very good for your back or overall health. They can also lead to unstable, rocky relationships.

*Multipurpose:* With more and more people choosing urban, apartment living, multipurpose beds are becoming increasingly popular. As convenient as they may be, however, beds that serve a dual purpose carry a hidden danger. We've already explained how storing objects under the bed can hinder your health (see page 32); turns out, beds with drawers can also lead to insomnia and a confused, complicated relationship.

*Feng Shui Solution:*

- If your bed has built-in drawers, only store sleep-related items, such as pajamas, blankets and sheets. No nostalgic photographs (especially of ex-lovers) allowed!

**Bed Placement**

You want your bedroom placed in the commanding position of your home, and you want your bed placed in the commanding position of your bedroom (see page 29).

If you can, position your bed as far from the bedroom door as possible. If you enter your room from the right, position the bed in the back left corner of the room. If your bedroom door is positioned left, place your bed in the far right. Should the entrance to your room be centered, then take your pick of either the back left or right corners. The commanding position affords you the best view of the room as well as a clear view of the bedroom door.

Remember the rule of twos. Don't back your bed into a corner; such an arrangement may impede your ability to find and maintain a successful relationship.

**Bed Height**

A bed that is too high can throw off your chances of finding a mate, while a bed that rests on, or barely off of, the ground can keep you in unhealthy relationships and block the flow of money into your life.

**Headboard**

A sturdy headboard is key to a stable love life. (By stable we don't mean unexciting, we mean long-lasting!) As discussed in the Career Chapter, a strong, solid headboard that's securely attached to the bed is best. Opt for one that is either upholstered or made from wood.

The shape of the headboard can also impact your love life. A square headboard encourages a harmonious relationship.

> Square signifies the earth element, drawing in stability and balance.

Rectangle represents Wood, and as such nurtures growth and expansion in your relationship.

Triangular headboards bring too much of the fire element into your relationship and can cause fights.

**Bed Dressing**

If your love life is stagnant, or if you've recently experienced a break-up (especially with a live-in partner), consider treating yourself to new sheets and a comforter. Texture counts…are you a silk, satin or cotton lover? When purchasing a comforter, try to implement some pinks and reds to stimulate romance and passion. Don't worry; it doesn't need to be girly with frills, flowers and hearts. A simple red duvet or sheets can usher in some passion. Or go natural with green, which can help bring in new love and an influx of cash.

> Pink helps open and heal your heart.

Don't go overboard on pillows. One for you, one for your partner, and no more than two decorative pillows to top it off. You want to leave some space for love, remember?

And ladies, leave off the stuffed teddy bears. Let's invite a real-life teddy bear into your bed, shall we?

### Time for a New Bed?

New beds bring in a clean, refreshed sweep of energy. It may be time for a major overhaul of your love life, and buying a brand new bed can be a love-saving cure. You might not need to take such a leap if a relationship ends, but if you've experienced a major illness, someone has died, you're moving into a new home, or you're left widowed, a new bed may be a safe bet.

We recommend against purchasing a used bed, which carries with it energy, emotions and stalemates from the previous owner's life.

Remember: An extremely effective overall cure for any bedroom issues is to hang a crystal from the center of the bedroom. Alternately, you can hang a crystal chandelier from the center of the room, as long as it is not directly over your bed.

### Cure with Color

Red stimulates the fire element and heats up your love life. Decorating with red curtains could be just the cure you need to spice things up in and out of the bedroom.

#### Paint Colors

Yellows and bright reds are too vibrant for the bedroom. Decorate instead with warm and seductive earth tones: chocolate, burgundy, dark and light neutrals, peaches, pinks, warm reds and plums. Avoid blues, greens, whites, grays and blacks, which are all too cool for bedroom walls.

You want to avoid the water element in the bedroom, so while a touch of blue won't have disastrous consequences, avoid blue in large amounts, like painting the walls blue!

### *Stimulate the Senses*

Aromatherapy can work wonders on your love life. Add some seduction into your life by diffusing a few drops of ylang-ylang essential oil in water and rub a drop or two onto your pillowcase.

Rose, jasmine, sandalwood, vanilla, neroli and lavender essential oils work just as well when it comes to adding a scent of passion to your boudoir. We highly recommend investing in an aromatherapy diffuser or oil warmer.

### *Create a Love Garden*

For those of you lucky enough to have a yard, we'd love for you to take advantage and create a love garden, to help love in your life bloom literally and metaphorically! Creating a love garden is highly personal. What colors and types of flowers and foliage inspire you? Traditionally, red, pink and yellow-bulbed flowers have been associated with love, but you can just as powerfully set your Intention with passionate blossoms of purple and blue. Surround your love garden with light, and add statues, figurines and crystals that represent the love you are seeking. You can also add a mini love garden to a balcony or patio…never feel limited in your opportunities to create love.

Hopefully, you're feeling lucky in love already! If you're single, already have a healthy dose of self-love, and are really just looking to draw in some romantic love, then take a look around your home to see if it's too gender specific. For instance, if you are a woman looking to attract a man, then consider toning down some of the frills so that he is not subconsciously threatened by all the yin energy. An easy fix is to add a painting of the sun to invite more yang energy into the space.

Likewise, if you're a man looking to invite a female into your life, and your home oozes masculinity, then bring some feminine energy into the space by adding a photograph or other pictorial element of the moon.

Love, like freedom, peace and justice, is an essential human right. When you are setting your Intention for love, remember that it is already a part of you, and you have the power to attract all the love that you desire.

❖ *Chapter Five* ❖

# YOUR FAMILY

Even if you're a happily single hermit with no interest in cultivating "family" in the traditional sense of the word, this is a not-to-be-missed chapter. Sure, family applies to our life partners, our children, our siblings, our parents, our grandparents and other relatives, but it also applies to our ancestral lineage and our communities. Amplifying harmony in the family area of your home not only uplifts the interpersonal relationships within your clan, but also expands and influences on a global scale.

**Career-driven folks take note:** the family area promotes harmony in your business family, so tending to this life area can greatly improve your work relationships, including your dealings with clients/customers.

We also dedicate this chapter to your children, both their positive growth and your relationship with them, and even include a special section on conception. But let's first bring more harmony into your interpersonal relationships by turning our attention to the family area, which, according to the Ba-Gua, is located in the left-center portion of your home.

## The Family Area

Once you've mapped out the family area, you're ready to combine powerful Intention with helpful feng shui cures. All it takes is some color creativity, some element magic and some inspiration-fueled symbols to help add harmony to hearth and home.

### Color Cure

The family area is matched with the colors green and blue. Let the vibrations of green calm and heal, while symbolically promoting growth, life and vitality in your family. Green is linked to Wood—the representative element of family. Whether aqua, ocean or indigo, blue stands in for the element Water, which nourishes Wood, thereby heightening family harmony.

Here are some suggestions for adding green and blue to the family area of your home, or to the family corner of any room in your house:

- Paint an accent wall green or blue.
- Add in come colorful, decorative pillows accented in greens and blues.

Add in a splash of black, which also represents Water.

- Add a green plant or a beautiful blue orchid to the family area.
- Adorn the walls with a painting of blues and greens.
- A vibrant green/blue bowl or vase perched on a coffee table is an elegant way to empower the family corner.
- A simple blue or green throw on the back of the sofa is an easy addition.

### Wood and Water

Wood cures bring a touch of spring to your life (the season associated with Wood), activating growth and expansion in all areas. A wood coffee table, bookshelf or other piece of wood furniture can easily infuse vitality and peace into your family. An easy cure to heal any fractions within the family is to frame family photographs in rectangular wooden frames and hang them in the family zone.

Water is a complementary element to Wood, and adding Water to the family area helps increase family harmony and flow. Add a table fountain or a photograph of moving water to accentuate free-flowing energy in your family.

*Fire and Metal in the Family Space*

The elements Fire and Metal can have unwelcome consequences on your interpersonal relationships if placed in the family areas of your home. Fire burns wood and metal cuts wood!

*Feng Shui Solution:*

- If your family corner is colored with high-energy oranges and reds, then it's time to redecorate. These colors add too much Fire!
- Got a fireplace in the family area? Negate the Fire by adding a painting of calm water. You could also add a mirror above the fireplace to weaken the effects of Fire.
- Metal has no place in the family zone, including family photographs framed in metal.

No family photos on the fireplace, including photos of your kids. It could lead to quarrels and tension among family members.

## The Living Room

When looking to accentuate family, special attention should be given to the place where your family gathers the most—the living room! What's the main purpose of a living room or den? Not to watch television, as evidenced by modern society, but as a gathering space for friends and family to relax, converse and connect. The living room is the contemporary version of our primitive ancestors' campfire circle, and just as important to survival today as it was back then. Care should be given to set a welcoming and comforting tone in your living room.

**Let's take a look at the ideal living room setup. Check all the boxes that apply to your home.**

❑   The living room is located at the front or center of the house and braced by at least two outside walls.

When visible from the front door, the living room welcomes both guests and free-flowing chi!

❑   There are no more than two doors in the living room.

❑   Sitting arrangements offer both guests and residents unobstructed views of the entryway.

❑   The entrance to the living room is not blocked by heavy furniture, such as the back of a couch.

❑   The living room is either square or rectangular in shape, and is not too small.

❑   The main sofa sits against a solid wall. This arrangement presents stability in all areas of your life, including family dynamics.

❑   Furniture is not placed under exposed beams.

❑   The television is not the focal point of the room.

Use a media cabinet to hide electronics when not in use, or position the TV diagonally in a corner so that it doesn't steal focus. Electronics contain active energy, so put them in life corners you wish to activate, like the fame and career areas.

❑   The living room is well lit.

Let's troubleshoot some common living room malfunctions.

*Back of Couch Faces the Entrance*

If the first thing you see upon entering your living room is the back of a couch, then rearranging your furniture is your primary feng shui fix. Remember, a clear view of the entryway from all seated positions is most desirable. If you absolutely cannot move the location of your sofa, then try to diffuse the negative impact with the following cures.

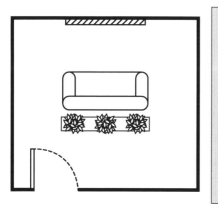

*Feng Shui Solution:*

- Add protection with a decorative table filled with vibrant green plants behind the sofa.
- Hang a mirror on the opposite wall to reflect the door.

**L-Shaped Sofas**

L-shaped sofas can introduce a poison arrow effect in the room, and for this reason are considered inauspicious. The L-shape can also create an unbalanced feeling in a room.

*Feng Shui Solution:*

- Hold off on buying a new sofa just yet. Add a plant at the end of the arrow section of the sofa to soften the impact.
- You can also hang a crystal ball from the ceiling.

## The Dining Room

While tied to our health and our wealth, the dining room also symbolizes connection between family members, and should be arranged accordingly. Entertaining also encourages networking, so if you're looking for a career boost, pay close attention!

### *The Dining Table*

The larger the dining table, the more auspicious your family and career life areas will be, but it's all relative to the space. Too large of a table in too small of a space becomes oppressive and destructive. Likewise, a dinky table in a large room may impede family dynamics.

The best shapes for dining tables include oval, circular, rectangular or square (with rounded corners). Round tables represent Metal, which is associated with gold or money. Dining tables made of oak, pine, cherry or walnut are preferable to dining tables made of glass or a chip board with veneer.

Chairs are also an important element. Opt for an even number of chairs, unless you have a circular table. Three chairs around a circular table are auspicious for those living alone. Chairs with a solid back are best.

Let's tackle an inauspicious dining room configuration.

### *The Dining Table Under a Beam*

When the dining table sits under a beam, conversation, career and cash flow can be stifled.

*Feng Shui Solution:*

- Move the table out from under the beam.
- Get creative and hide the beam, either by painting it the same color as the ceiling or adding beautiful greens of ivy to its bottom. Let your artistic side emerge and paint on the blooming vines.

A warm rug colored in earth-inspired hues underneath the dining table helps ground the space and stimulate conversation and communication among family members.

### Use It, Don't Lose It!

One of the main challenges a dining room faces is its lack of use, as well as its abuse as an "anything goes" room. Avoid treating the dining room like a dumping ground for mail, kids' backpacks, shopping bags, etc. Keep the space clean and clutter free.

The dining room can also suffer from inactivity. If you live alone and rarely use your dining room, then make a concerted effort to spend some time with it. Tote your laptop to the dining room table and get some work done. Invite a friend over for tea, or use it for game night, homework or crafting. Just be sure to clean up when you're done.

## The Children's Corner (or Cultivating Creativity)

The children area of your home impacts the health, well-being and growth of your children. It is also linked to creativity and communication, so if you are looking to cultivate creative endeavors and activate your artistic side, then spend some time nurturing the children corner. Cultivating creativity can help the writer remove writer's block, the mathematician solve a difficult equation and the lawyer craft compelling and winning arguments.

Located at the center right of the Ba-Gua, the children area sits directly across from the family area. The color white is associated with the children area and can be incorporated in many different cures. For instance, if your home is L-shaped and you are missing the children area, you can fill in the missing section by planting white flowers where the children section of the house should be.

Here are some suggestions for activating your children/creativity area:

- Add Metal: this could be in the form of metal-framed photos of your children, metal works of art or metal furniture.
- Add artwork that speaks to you of creativity, but avoid fire and water colors!

Fire and Water dampen creativity and can impede your child's progress.

- This section of your home is the perfect place to put your kids' artwork on display.
- Add some earth element into the mix by implementing the color yellow, as well as Earth's geometric shapes—square, rectangle and cube.
- Appropriate paint colors for the children area are associated with Metal and Earth: white, gray, sand, yellow and other muted earth tones.
- Add a game, like Chess or Checkers, to inspire childlike creativity and fun.

- Electronics are welcome in this corner of your home or room. They activate energy!
- Add a vase of white, blooming flowers to amp up the creativity.

Avoid:

- Fireplaces in the children area. (See cure on page 112.)
- No fire elements, like reds and candles.
- Avoid strong blues, which can lead to restless minds when placed in the children area.
- Triangular, pyramid-shaped objects should not be placed in the creativity corner, as they are associated with Fire.

## Your Child's Room

Your child's room is best placed in—you guessed it—the children area. Children's rooms are also favorably located in the front of the house. Less ideal are kids' rooms positioned in the center of the home, or farther back than the master bedroom. This inopportune layout can result in the child becoming "master" of the home. When a child sleeps in the bedroom that is farthest in the back of the house, he is given more of a commanding position. To remedy, switch bedrooms, or hang a large mirror at the front of the house in direct line with the child's bed. This pulls the child's energy back to the front of the house, so you can regain control of your household.

*Child's Room Bigger than the Master Bedroom*

This setup also tilts the balance of power in favor of the child. The child might exhibit hyperactivity or unruly tendencies.

---

*Feng Shui Solution:*

◆ Switch bedrooms.
◆ Hang a metal wind chime outside the child's door and a crystal sphere in the center of the master bedroom.

---

### Bed Placement

Your child's bed position is just as important as yours. To ensure your child's safety and progress, either place the bed in the children area (center right) or in the commanding position (see page 29). Placing the bed in the children area is especially ideal for stimulating intellect, strength and energy. All the rules for beds apply: strong solid headboard placed against a sturdy wall, ideally not underneath a window, not in direct line of the door, etc. To solve any misaligned elements, such as a beam over the bed or a slanted ceiling, refer to Chapter 1 pages 34-37.

### Bed Rules

Kids outgrow beds almost as quickly as they outgrow clothes. Don't hang on to beds that your kids have gotten too big for. Otherwise, growth could be stunted…and not just physical! Test scores could start faltering, and emotional maturity could stall.

#### Multifunctional Beds and Bunk Beds

Day beds, futons and trundles can foster feelings of instability and erratic energy by way of their "temporary" nature. You should also say goodbye to bunk beds, with can suffocate a child's energy and health.

Symptoms can manifest as emotional immaturity and possible personality disorders.

*Feng Shui Solution:*

* Swap out a bunk bed for a single bed (or two).
* Hang two crystals (or similarly charged protective amulets) above each child's sleeping position. One will be hung from the ceiling, the other from the bottom of the top bunk.
* To help negate any less-than-ideal bed setups, place green plants in the bedroom to enliven chi.

**Colors for Kids**

Children's rooms do best in white, blues and greens. Use a combination of colors, as rooms with more than one primary color help increase a child's brain function and develop sensory faculties. If your child is hyperactive, then add some darker neutral-toned colors to calm him/her down.

Here are some specific enhancement cures:

* For a stronger intellect, add a bright light to the children area of the room.
* For balanced emotions, hang a crystal over the head of the bed.
* To enrich awareness and cognitive abilities, hang a wind chime in the knowledge area of the home.

# Cures for Conception

Looking to increase the size of your family? All the feng shui principles discussed thus far affect your ability to conceive. A healthy amount of chi running freely through your home is affected by everything from a dirty, cluttered front entrance, to a leaky faucet that is dripping away your life energy…and that of your unborn child! So, follow the suggested cures and add the conception tricks below for a fertility boost.

- Enhance the children area with baby symbols. You can frame a photograph of a child that resembles you and your partner, or add a fluffy teddy bear stuffed with your Intention!
- Add some traditional Chinese fertility symbols to the bedroom: elephants, dragons, double fish, rabbits, pomegranates, eggs, a single piece of hollow bamboo and red paper lanterns.
- If you want to get real traditional, put a bowl of uncooked rice under the bed.

Remember not to sweep under the bed or rearrange your bedroom furniture…the ancient Chinese believed doing so could frighten away the soul of your unborn child! And don't deaden intimacy or conception with electronics in your bedroom.

In order to assess any blocked chi, use the Chi Checklist below:

### Chi Checklist

- No obstructed doors or windows. No barriers, boxes or furniture blocking the flow of chi through any room.
- All rooms are free of clutter.
- The house is clean (stick to a regular cleaning and maintenance schedule).
- Dishes aren't piled up in the sink.

- Sinks, tubs, toilets, stoves and light fixtures are all clean and in working condition.
- Windows are clean both inside and out.
- No burnt out light bulbs or malfunctioning equipment.
- Plants are all healthy and well tended.
- Sharp corners have been neutralized with feng shui cures.
- Main entrance is well lit and inviting.

## Your Family's Safety

We felt that a discussion of safety was best placed in the Family Chapter. Do not work with protective feng shui measures in a spirit of fear, but rather from a place of acknowledgement that there are many elements in this world that can have an adverse effect on us, and should be kept far from the home.

For added protection implement the following.

### *Sturdy Front Door*

A strong front door offers obvious protection, both physically and psychologically. Again, you'll want an unblocked flow of energy, which means a clutter-free porch and driveway. The front door should be well cared for—no squeaking hinges, chipped paint, unused nails or winter holiday wreaths in March! Same principles hold true for windows. All should be sturdy, well kept and in working order.

Draw in some positive, protective chi with a bright welcome mat at the front door.

## Neighborly Relations

Sometimes, despite our best efforts, things can get tense with neighbors. This tension often doesn't stop at the property line but spills into our homes. If you are experiencing problems with neighbors, implement the following cures.

*Feng Shui Solution:*

- A traditional cure is to hang a Ba-Gua mirror over the front door on the outside. This will neutralize negative energy.
- To add the mirror element, add some mirror balls (witches balls) to your garden. They help to push back any negative energy you may be receiving from neighbors.
- Add protective energy with a beautiful fence to draw parameters between your energy and theirs—or create a fence made from tall evergreen shrubs.
- If the tension emanates from a specific area, then add a rock garden to that space to diffuse energy.
- Hang a wind chime at the property line between the two houses (or apartments).

**A word about the Ba-Gua mirror:** A concave mirror will absorb the negative energy, neutralizing it before it can enter your home. A convex Ba-Gua on the other hand, bounces back the negative energy, which isn't as effective as ridding of the negative altogether!

## Crystal Protection

Crystals are naturally infused with Earth's protective properties, and as such can give an added layer of protection to your physical person or your home. Dark, smoky crystals are great for ensuring safety. Try: black tourmaline, black onyx, black obsidian, hematite, tiger's eye, smoky quartz and ammonite.

### *The Energy of Essential Oils*

Protect your home further by diffusing essential oils in an aromatherapy diffuser. Use woody oils like cypress, juniper, pine, frankincense, myrrh, cinnamon and sandalwood. If you prefer more flowery scents, try lilac and rose geranium.

Securing your home with just a few of these improvements will help your family life area, and every aspect of your life.

❖ *Chapter Six* ❖

# CONGRATULATIONS!

You've explored the vast world of feng shui and hopefully found a few easy tips to try out in your home. Remember to listen to your inner feng shui consultant. Be aware of the energy swirling in your environment and tap into how certain objects and colors and arrangements make you feel as you are deciding on cures.

*Feng Shui on a Dime* recommends a little at a time. If you try too many cures at once, it's difficult to know what works and what may accidentally be impeding progress. Of course, if your home needs a major overhaul (*think: de-clutter, cleaning and maintenance*) then start with that first! Then decide the life area that warrants the most attention and go from there. Chances are when that's improved, the other areas of your life will fall in line.

May the feng shui solutions in this book draw the three Great Blessings your way: Health, Happiness and Prosperity. Here's to a life of health, wealth, love, peace and abundance!